# Devil in the Mirror: Overcoming the Enemy's Attack

By

C. Nathaniel Brown

Atlanta, GA

Devil in the Mirror: Overcoming the Enemy's Attack



C. Nathaniel Brown

EX3

Cover design: Mitchell Coles, Colestyle Designs



Library of Congress Cataloging-in-Publication Data

Brown, C. Nathaniel (Charles), 1971-

Devil in the Mirror: Overcoming the Enemy's Attack

Expected End Entertainment/EX3Books

ISBN 978-0-9885545-0-4 (pbk)

# DEDICATION

This book is dedicated to you for desiring to get the devil out of your mirror and to those who perished while many of us were in the process.

# TABLE OF CONTENTS


| | |
|---|---|
| Acknowledgments | 7 |
| Introduction | 9 |
| Counseling the Devil | 11 |
| 2,000-Step Process | 13 |
| Five Requests to be Blessed | 19 |
| Trials and Tribulations | 33 |
| Know Who You Are | 39 |
| The Devil Wants You or What You Have | 45 |
| Know Your Enemy | 49 |
| The Devil in the Mirror | 67 |
| Identifying the Demons | 85 |
| Deciding to Deal with the Demons | 99 |
| Defeating the Enemy | 107 |

Spiritual Warfare: Getting the Devil out the Mirror 111

My Process 133

Beware the Premature Celebration 139

Net Losses, Net Gains 147

Recovering What was Lost 159

Giving God What's His 167

# Acknowledgments

This book is the representation of a journey that God guided me on to reach out to people who looked in the mirror one day, saw the devil and decided they needed Jesus to rescue them. You're not alone in your struggle for wholeness. Now you have some help.

I thank God for being who He is and what He is in my life. I thank Him for using me to get glory. Many people have asked to be used by God and when He used them, they bailed on Him. I thank Him for helping me stand so that He can get more glory from you as you read this book.

I would like to acknowledge my wife, Tammie, for her strength through difficult times. To my children, Brittnie and Bradley, I love you. To My Dude, Kyan, wow! My parents, Ellen Brown and Tim Harris and Tyrone and Gloria Kemp (RWG), thank you for unconditional love and your countless examples.

And to everyone who was there for me in my time of need whether through prayer, through a touch, a phone call, or a smile, I love you and bless you. Much love and many blessings to you, who picked up this book and desire to overcome the enemy's attack in your life. I thank you for allowing me to share with you what God has done and is doing in my life.

# INTRODUCTION

This is a love story. I wouldn't necessarily call it love at first sight, but there's something special about falling in love and knowing that there's nothing in the world or outside the world that can convince you otherwise. That's what happened to me as I discovered that Jesus loves me with an unconditional love and invited me to love Him in a more intimate way—despite my not having the same capacity to love the way He does.

Maybe some things you read won't sound like love, but it was love that allowed this to come to fruition. It's going to be love that causes your heart to feel as you read further and love that helps you to heal.

See, there is a unique foundation of love that the Bible describes when it says that God so loved the world that He gave His only son, that whosoever believes in Him shall have everlasting life (John 3:16). That's love. I thought I knew that love when I accepted Jesus into my life and all my past sins were forgiven and I began a relationship with the one who was, who is and who is to come.

But a funny thing happened. I didn't consider that I would need to know Him in a greater way because of sins of commission and sins of omission. There were some things that God had to teach me:

1. To understand a deeper love.
2. To learn how to love Him in a way that He would receive my sacrifice but more importantly that I would remain obedient.
3. To identify the enemy and his antics.
4. To examine myself.
5. To protect the foundation so the rest of the building wouldn't fall.

   For me, that foundation was love and it remains love.

I looked in the mirror and saw something that disgusted me. That's when I determined that no matter what, I would rid the devil from my mirror. The next time I looked into that mirror, I wanted to see God and God only. I wanted to see love. That was the journey I began that day.

That can be the journey you begin today.

# Counseling the Devil

Counseling the devil landed me in jail. It could have cost me my life, but I was spared in the natural. But the closing of that cell door behind me in 2004 symbolized another death, the culmination of weight the enemy held over my family and me as we fought to live. It was buried in a cold cell, 214 Pod 4A at the Allegheny County Jail.

Farewell to the most difficult time in my life and welcome to the devil being exposed, God being glorified and my family and I celebrating the victory as we pursue our God-given purpose.

I got the title, *Devil in the Mirror: Overcoming the Enemy's Attack*, as I submitted to the process that God placed me in to make sure that I was indeed becoming the man that He called me to be. I had to go through some things. I had to see some things. I had to feel some things. I had to lose some things. In other words, I had to die. That was personal. I wrote about how at 30, God gave me a message I thought I was only to teach or preach. But it was much more than a message for the people. It was a message for me.

To briefly summarize, God asked, "What would you do if you only had 3½ years to live?" It was deep. I began to study the

3½-year public ministry of Jesus Christ. I didn't realize then that in 3½ years I would die and need the power of God to resurrect me. The devil thought I was a pawn in his game, but what the devil meant for evil God turned for good. God used the devil to get glory. But in doing so, it takes exposing each one of us, the devils in us, the flaws in our character, in our ministries, and Satan himself. When the devil's plan backfires, sometimes we get hit by some of the pellets and sustain flesh wounds. But the devil absorbs the severe injuries, severe unto death. We live to tell the stories. This is one of them. chapter one text here.

# A 2000-Step Process

When Thomas Edison invented the light bulb, a reporter asked him, how did it feel to fail a seemingly insurmountable amount of times before finally discovering the correct formula to getting the light to come on? Edison's reply was simple. He said he never failed. It was simply a 2,000-step process.

The same can be said for many of us as we try to discover the perfect relationship with Jesus Christ. As simple as it seems to us today to grab a light bulb from Isle 10 in the grocery store, bring it home and screw it in and we have light, it was a much more complicated process before it was perfected. We tend to take for granted things that appear easy so we fail to work at it, never getting out of it what was intended.

Gospel singer Donnie McClurkin sang a song that became such a popular anthem for both Christians and non-Christians, that it could be heard on secular radio stations as much as Christian stations. The controversial song, entitled, *We Fall Down*, simply says, "We fall down, but we get up. For a saint is just a sinner who fell down and got up."

Some people disliked the song because it gave the

impression that Christians have no strength and it minimized the keeping power of Jesus. They said it gave people the right to willingly transgress and fall from the will of God because of the assurance of getting back up again.

I got sick of hearing the song, but I heard in the song that it might be a 2,000-step process before you get it right. Just don't give up.

Take, for example, the blind beggar in Luke 18 who was sitting by the roadside when Jesus and the disciples entered Jericho. Despite being rebuked by the disciples and the crowd, the beggar began shouting to Jesus to have mercy on him. Jesus asked him what he wanted and the beggar said he wanted to see. Jesus told the beggar, *"Receive your sight; your faith has healed you."* (v.42) The Bible said *immediately* he received his sight and followed Jesus.

We don't know how long this particular man had been without sight or how long he had been searching for healing. We know the woman with the issue of blood had been trying for 12 years to find a cure, but doctors didn't have what she needed. It wasn't until she received from Jesus that she got her healing. The lame man at the pool of Bethesda had been an invalid for 38 years before he got what he needed. The point is, these three and numerous other examples in the Bible prove that sometimes it is an extended process that comes in God's time, not ours. Jesus tells a blind man he healed that neither he nor his parents sinned to cause the blindness, but *"this happened so that the work of God might be displayed in his life."* (John 9:3)

Likewise, we have to remain *in* the process because quitting at 1,999 will keep us from the blessing we stand to receive if we let patience work her perfect will in us. We do ourselves an injustice and can nullify the miracles that God wants to perform in our lives if we quit. Imagine if the lame man wouldn't have been by the pool that particular day. Apparently no one helped him into the pool for 38 years when the healing power was flowing through the waters. I'm sure there were times that he almost lost hope and wanted to give up, but there was something driving him to continue in the faith, that one day he would receive his healing.

That's a message that many people hear, yet it escapes the depths of their hearts because they choose not to hold on. I counseled a suicidal woman who quickly became hopeless when doctors couldn't determine a blood issue that she suffered with for years. Doctors tried to medicate her on several occasions to thin the blood, then cause the blood to clot, then to regulate her blood pressure. She felt like it was such an unending cycle that she'd be better off dead.

She had heard the stories about the issues of blood and believed for healing on several occasions only to find the problem returned. But in the end, she came to the conclusion that nothing she tried worked, so she'd really turn the situation over to Jesus and wait. The woman never got healed from the disease, but she found peace in the process and eventually had her medication regulated to the point she no longer suffered or had frequent visits to the doctor.

Tammie often rides me about starting so many projects and never finishing them. Sometimes I tried new business ventures, such as network marketing or real estate, or read self-help books, or subscribed to magazines with new ideas, hoping one of them would be my open door to the next level of success. Oftentimes, the ventures didn't turn out the way that I envisioned them, but I never saw them as failures (okay, except for the real estate exploration).

For example, it was my foray into network marketing that I discovered that God was calling me to preach. I'll never forget a regional conference I attended for this particular telecommunication company in which national motivational speakers Zig Ziglar and Les Brown were guest speakers. I was standing in the middle of about 8,000 people just like me, wanting to become the next millionaire produced through network marketing. People stood on chairs, screaming and chanting the name of the their local marketing groups, as Zig Ziglar told the crowd that today they were on their way to changing the history and future of their families. Les Brown told the crowd that the difference between people who have and people who don't is that one chooses to go after what he wants and the other simply talks about it.

I remember thinking to myself, "That's what I want to do. I want to motivate people to believe that they can achieve whatever they set their minds and hearts to. I want to help people go from where they are to where they want to be." It was some time later that I realized I was saying, "That's what the word of God does. I could be a conduit for God's message. I could have an impact."

Becoming a conduit for God also became a process that included schooling, training and sitting and observing leaders that God put in authority over me. I could have pulled out of that process and never witnessed God using me for His glory the same way that Zig Ziglar motivated the people at that conference. I have witnessed healings, deliverance and people becoming believers because I decided to remain in the process even when times got hard. People lived because I decided to die.

If we witnessed God's hand of mercy and love in seasons

of sunshine, we should also remain in the process when we're coming out of a situation where it feels we're in between a rock and a hard place, so to speak. I'll share later the story of how I had to endure the poking and burning as God was purifying me during my most recent 2,000-step process. It included my arrest on charges of indecent assault, my acquittal, the deliverance process, coming clean about the hell I went through, my role in exposing the devil and becoming the man God called me to be.

# Five Requests to be Blessed

I've been involved in a lot of fights in my life growing up in the inner city of Baltimore. Back then, we put a leaf or piece of paper on our shoulder and if the person that wanted to fight you knocked it off, you'd throw blows or wrestle until a winner was declared. I rarely fought clean because I was usually smaller than the person I was to fight. So it was no surprise that I'd pick up a bottle, a brick or my favorite, a baseball bat.

We'd fight for neighborhoods, money, girls, and family.

As time went on, fights went from one-on-one to group fights to utilizing knives and guns. Whatever you had that would help you, you used.

Well, I found myself recently in the battle of my life against the devil and his servants. So I had to fight for my neighborhood, money, my girl, my family, and everything that I had. Not only did I need to battle the enemy, I wrestled with God and struggled with myself. The well-respected minister, basketball coach and newspaper reporter had turned into a menace in the sight of the public and drew the ire of everyone around him, including his family. I sought the Lord about the battle, my enemy and the weapons I should use to win this fight and he revealed to me 5 Requests to be Blessed. I want to share them with you so that you, too, can be equipped for the battle you are in or prepared for the battle that is to come. Remember, that even your battle can be a 2,000-step process. So even if it doesn't appear that your enemy is retreating, continue to press forward. You might be as close as Step 1,999.

## I. Salvation/Holy Spirit

Accepting Jesus Christ as your personal Lord and Savior is the first step in being blessed. Without this initial step, you are making your reservations for defeat, spending your eternity in hell and having everything stolen from you, being killed and destroyed. (John 10:10)

The Bible instructs us in Romans 10:9-10 that if we confess with our mouths and believe in our hearts that Jesus is Lord and that God raised him from the dead, we secure our reservations for heaven. In conjunction with the decision to invite Jesus to rule over our eternity, God offers us a gift in the person of the Holy Spirit that will lead and guide us during our time here on earth.

When Jesus went back to heaven to sit on the throne with the Father and make intercession for us, He said that He would leave us a Comforter, the help that we need to realize that no matter what happens we are not alone.

In other words, we have to choose whose side we're on, which army we're fighting for.

## II. Wisdom

Wisdom is defined as accumulated knowledge or enlightenment; utilizing knowledge and experience with common sense and insight; a spiritual path that functions to release our minds from delusions or their imprints; the ability to apply spiritual truth to a specific issue in an especially relevant fashion; to make proper choices in different situations, based on sufficient information.

I had to include this in-depth definition of wisdom so that we can have a complete understanding that wisdom is more than simply knowing something. I like two particular parts of that definition—a spiritual path that functions to release our minds from delusions or their imprints and making proper choices in different situations, based on sufficient information.

How many times have you been caught up in situations because you didn't provide yourself a spiritual path that released your mind from delusions? How many times have you thought to yourself, "I can handle this"? Or maybe you used the way of escape that God provided you once before and found yourself in the same situation and thought, “If I did it once, I can do it again?” That might be the imprint of the delusions setting you up for a fall. It doesn’t take much room for a fall.

Oftentimes, we make improper decisions because we don’t have sufficient information. We find ourselves trying to dig out of a hole because we thought we knew enough to make a decision but actually made the decision while in a state of delusion and far from having the wisdom that God is our deliverer.

I had to learn that the hard way. I was under a state of great delusion feeling I was doing the right thing in counseling the devil, but little did I know it was based on insufficient information. As a result, I got sucked into the enemy’s web of unwise untruths intended to steal, kill and destroy me, my family, the church and the reputation and witness of the Savior Himself. So it became obvious in that intimate time with God that wisdom was lacking. More importantly it was needed and available.

God said that Solomon asked for a good thing when he prayed for wisdom. (I Kings 3) He could have asked for silver, gold, women, slaves, more power or even cattle on a thousand hills. But Solomon got the revelation that with God-given wisdom, he would possess the weapon that could lead to the things he wanted and needed. Because he asked for something that pleased God, God gave him riches and honor, a long life and favor in the sight of man.

I Kings 4:29-34 says:

*"God gave Solomon wisdom and very great insight, and a breadth of understanding as measureless as the sand on the seashore. Solomon's wisdom was greater than the wisdom of all the men of the east, and greater than all the wisdom of Egypt. He was wiser than any other man, including Ethan the Ezrahite—wiser than Heman, Calcol and Darda, the sons of Mahol. And his fame spread to all the surrounding nations. He spoke three thousand proverbs and his songs numbered a thousand and five. He described plant life, from the cedar of Lebanon to the hyssop that grows out of walls. He also taught about animals and birds, reptiles and fish. Men of all nations came to listen to Solomon's wisdom, sent by all the kings of the world, who had heard of his wisdom."*

So you can understand why God told me to ask for wisdom. I would admonish you to do the same.

## III. Purpose

After wisdom, seek your divine purpose. There is more to the battle than victory. We've already come to understand that the battle really isn't ours, but the Lord is fighting the battle. So if we have committed to the process, whether it's one-step, 12-steps, or 2,000 steps, there is purpose in it, through it and after it.

Take, for example, Operation Iraqi Freedom. Whether you agreed or disagreed with the decision to go to war in the Middle East, our former Commander-in-Chief President George W. Bush and his staff had said that the purpose of the battle was to free Iraq from dictatorship and to begin the process of ridding the world of terrorism. Once they engaged in battle, they decided they were not going to stop until that purpose was fulfilled to their satisfaction.

People had called for the United States to pull out of Iraq and other countries because of insufficient information about Iraq, the terrorists and the dangers that our troops faced. The stance that President Bush and his staff took was that they would see the process through because there was purpose in it, through it and after it.

That's what we have to do. Not everyone is going to agree with you when you make your decision to pursue your purpose. Some people might think that you're crazy. Others might think you have ulterior motives. And yet others might leave you alone because they can't understand what you've been through, where you are or where you're going. But that's totally okay because God needs to get you in a place where it's just you and Him in the war room strategizing.

It is in that place of intimacy that God can reveal to you that there is an anticipated outcome that should guide your actions. He'll tell you that *this* should be your primary focus or *that* should be your reason for existence.

I've been on both sides of the prayer for purpose, as He revealed to me in an intimate setting of 8,000 people that He was calling me to preach His word, to motivate and encourage and to help people obtain salvation, healing, and deliverance. He was calling me to minister to His people, something I never imagined I would do. On the other side, I was fighting to maintain my relationship with Him, keep my marriage, restore my family and again find favor in the sight of my church family. I had to depend on God's instructions on what I should ask Him for. I could no longer trust myself and I had no one else to turn to.

So when you get in that intimate place and begin to petition God, or He asks you what you want, don't forget to include purpose.

## IV. Favor

One of my favorite scriptures is Proverbs 22:1, which says, *"A good name is rather to be chosen rather than great riches, and loving favor rather than silver and gold."*

In a lot of ways, favor is in the same class with wisdom because favor will bring about the things that the Word says are secondary, at best. Favor, defined as an advantage or benefit to someone or something because of gracious kindness, can lead a king to bestow everything he has to you. Ask Joseph. Favor can cause you and your seed to be blessed for generations. Ask Abraham. Favor will hand your enemies over to you without casualties to your camp. Ask Joshua.

God loves favor because it's one of the times when no one can take credit for what He's done. I believe that's why He instructed me to pray for favor. There were some issues deep in the crevices of my mind and heart that no one knew but God. I could have asked for help from man and maybe he could have helped with some surface issues, but there's no way that man's favor could have placed the right people in my life at the right time. Don't get me wrong; God uses man's favor also to show us that there is a level of trust and understanding that we must have one to another. But in some cases, especially in the midst of battle, God's favor is the only one that can present the kind of gracious kindness and advantage that can bring us from the gutter to the throne.

Once He is pleased that we have requested favor and

began to receive His loving favor, then He can transfer some favor to earthly vessels to bestow the love of God to us. I learned that when I didn't think God would use a human being because of the isolation I found myself in.

I remember God revealing to me that He would have people give me money as a sign that His favor was upon me. A week later, I attended a local church service. At offering time, the minister received a special offering and asked people to pass their money down to the left and an usher would pick it up from the person at the end of the pew. I was the person everyone passed money to and God said again, "This is a sign." At another service, I went to place my offering on the altar and almost everybody I walked past handed me money to take to the altar. God repeated, "This is a sign." Another day, a friend pulled his car next to mine, rolled down his window and handed me money to buy lunch. Another friend said God told him to pay his tithes to me, much like Abraham paid his tithes to Melchizedek in the Bible. It reaffirmed to me that God still thought highly of me and that He was releasing favor to me. If you are a regular person who has yet to ask for favor and receive it, this might not mean anything to you. But to the extraordinary people who understand the building of your faith when God makes a promise to you, you're rejoicing with me. You understand that I've given the examples of the seeds that were planted. It's not important to give all the examples of how the seeds grew. What's important is to know that favor has small and large blessings both from God and from those He's placed on earth whose calling includes blessing you. They're waiting for you to ask God to release favor so they can fulfill their purpose.

You'll learn more later about God's favor during my trial.

## V. Life and Family Life

Listen to this. Esther, a Jewish woman, found herself in the royal court as the wife of King Xerxes. Not only had she found favor in God's eyes and the king's eyes, she had gained a revelation of what her purpose was and based on wisdom, she knew what to ask when faced with a situation that could have changed the history of a race of people.

Because she had found favor in the king's sight, he asked her, *"...what is your petition? It will be given you. What is your request? Even up to half the kingdom, it will be granted. Then Queen Esther answered, 'If I have found favor with you, O king, and if it pleases your majesty, grant me my life—this is my petition. And spare my people—this is my request. For I and my people have been sold for destruction and slaughter and annihilation."* (Esther 7:2c-4a)

Maybe you're reading this and you're thinking to yourself, "This is a given." I applaud you. But not everyone is in that place. Remember the young lady I counseled that was suicidal? Well, that was just one example of the people that I've come across that simply didn't desire to live anymore and couldn't care less for the lives of others.

Maybe you're one of those people right now, contemplating whether you should end your life because it seems like nothing is going in your favor. God wants you to know that you can make it, that you're special to Him and that you're special to other people. God's word tells us that in our weakness, He is strong. Beyond that, you'd be surprised how important you are to others, even in your down times. Life wouldn't be the same without you.

One of the tricks of the enemy is to deceive us into thinking we're all alone and that nobody cares whether we live or die or that things will be better for others if we were dead. That's because the enemy has no life. I realized this prior to my most recent battle so I didn't face suicide as a possibility. However, there was a time that I did. As brief as the thought was, it wouldn't have taken much for me to end it all and think that I was doing the right thing. Once again, that's the delusion of the mind that prevents us from making wise decisions. That's why it's important to ask for these requests in conjunction with one another.

Imagine, if you will, that Abraham decided to end his life. The word said that the seed of Abraham, Jesus Christ himself, was to come into the world and save the world from sin. But Abraham, like Esther, decided that he wanted life and life for his family. As a result, we now can access the blessings of God that comes with life. Jesus wants us to have life and life more abundantly.

When I was faced with this request, I put my all into it because life is special to me. I know God has more purpose for me than meets the eye and I want to fulfill everything that He's called me to do. Likewise, I want my family to live. I wanted us to be a family, despite our shortcomings and bad decisions and occasionally being deceived by the enemy. One thing I'm sure of is that God granted life for my family and me. And I know that He can do it for you and your family. Remember, there is a difference between existing and living.

## Other requests

This is in no way an exhaustive list of requests to be blessed. However, these are five that God led me to in my time of need. They have helped me become more intimate with God, hear clearer from Him, overcome the battles that I face and better pursue the daily ministry that God has placed before me. I pray that you use them to help you along your way and that they will be a blessing to everyone who comes in contact with the new you.

Through prayer and fasting for these five and other God-inspired requests, you will be found pleasing in God's sight, honored among men and establish righteous seed of your own in the earth.

# TRIALS AND TRIBULATIONS

## Heading Toward a Trial

When I met with my attorney not long after posting bond, I learned about the extent of the media attempting to reach my family and church leadership for comment. It pained me to know that my family had to deal with that circus because of me. I told my attorney, Bob Del Greco, to contact the District Attorney's office to offer a plea – no contest on the initial count of indecent assault with two years of unsupervised probation. I wanted an end to the horror that was taking place in my life, my family's life, the church and everyone connected to me. I didn't want any more reporters knocking on my in-laws' doors. I didn't want people pretending to console my son as if they cared about any of us. I didn't want my church family to have to rehearse saying, "No comment," as camera crews bombarded them before and after services. I wanted my wife to return to a normal life and not have to worry about who was looking at her weird or who was genuine when they told her they were praying for her and me. I was anxious to get to the church leadership and apologize for the position I put them in and for letting them down. I had words prepared from the depths of my heart for the church members who needed me yet I was out of place. I couldn't shake not being with my friends because the case was unresolved and what had been circulated were rumors, lies and speculation. But I didn't want to put any of them in a bad situation where they would have strife in their marriages because of me. I wanted so badly to sit down with Bishop Carswell to comfort my spiritual dad, to explain in more detail what had happened and to share how much it hurt me to know the pain and grief I caused him. I was ready to talk to my family and friends outside of Pittsburgh but I was concerned someone was monitoring telephone conversations. Plus, Del Greco had already advised me not to talk to many people about anything until there was some resolution. On top of all that, I didn't want the case to proceed to trial because things that would have come out could have further hurt people in my life and exposed other people and their families, creating an avalanche of chaos.

The no contest plea would have allowed me to bring resolution to the matter so that I could move forward with my life. It would have meant all of the other areas and people that I was concerned about could also move on. At the time, I was comfortable with that decision, despite Del Greco asking me numerous times if I were sure. He was the first person who had gotten details about the relationship, the set-up and the intricacies of the case. He was confident that we would prevail. I believed that as well, but that wasn't where my heart was. My heart yearned for others to heal. So I was willing to plead no contest to indecent assault because I would bring closure to the case without admitting guilt. (The sentencing guideline for a no contest plea, however, is the same as a guilty verdict in a jury or non-jury trial.)

By the time Del Greco got back to me with a response from the assistant district attorney, I had grown weary of a lot of people I had been trying to protect. I was more concerned about everybody else, which isn't out of the ordinary. But for the first time, I was beginning to feel like people that I was for were against me. I felt so alone. Those changes, coupled with the assistant district attorney's arrogance and unwillingness to consider my offer, created a battle mentally that I had never had before.

Her response to my offer? An emphatic no! Her offer? Plead guilty to two counts of indecent assault, serve four years of supervised probation and enroll in a sex offenders therapy program. Del Greco knew my answer immediately and we were headed toward a trial.

## Tribulations

Tribulation is a period of great affliction, trial, distress or suffering. I had become familiar with this term and all that accompanied it. Some people felt that I deserved to be miserable and suffer great affliction because God provided ways of escape that I didn't take. It was okay to them that I was in a state of distress and depression. I was learning what lepers experienced being on the outside looking in. I was hurt, wounded, and dying and at times I couldn't find anyone to speak life into me. This period of my life was scarred and marred.

A lot of people were unaware of the death threats I received. They didn't know about the articles, blogs and websites that posted pictures and terroristic-type threats against me. I saw the local papers and newscasts that had broken me down to nothing. I heard the radio commentary that called me everything but a child of God. I'll never forget sitting in jail watching the news in the common area of the pod when a report came on about me and my case. Another inmate did a double take. He looked at me and asked me if that was me. I just nodded my head in shame. A couple other inmates' cases were also on the news that days and to them it was a badge of honor. One gave another a high five and said, "You famous son!" I was sick to my stomach. I could only imagine what was taking place outside the jail walls as my family and friends watched the same newscasts.

I thought about the Tribulation that the Bible speaks of, the seven-year period when the Anti-Christ arises to power, bringing with him trials and tribulations. Persecution of the saints will be commonplace. There will be life and death decisions to be made in the midst of war, disease, apostasy, sin and self-mutilation. I also remembered that the Tribulation is a precursor for the Millennial Reign of Christ. So for those who choose to endure the trials and tribulation, there indeed will be a reward to grasp.

It's most difficult, however, to hold fast to such beliefs when your prior belief system has been shattered during the trials and tribulations that have ultimately come to edify you. You had hope in a pastor and he let you down. You had hope in a friend and she let you down. You had faith in promises that weren't fulfilled. You had faith in love that turned to hate. You had strength in your courage to stand yet you fell. You had confidence in your ability to overcome yet you were temporarily conquered.

Tribulations bring you to crossroads. You are faced with split decisions and must determine which way you will go, unsure of what lies ahead. But when that decision is made, you find yourself willingly accepting the challenges and/or blessings to come. Either the tribulations make you or they break you.

I've been bent a few times during the tribulations of my life, including the period I experienced public humiliation. But I was determined not to break. I longed for the day that I would look myself in the face and know that I had endured the enemy's attack. I wanted to stand face-to-face with my adversary and say that I have overcome his latest barrage of fiery darts and have become a better person. I wanted to seek the presence of my God clean, pure and shining. I desired to come through the refiner's fire, be purified through the process, and I wanted to be the finest silver and gold instruments that God created. (Malachi 3:3) I envisioned offering Him me. But who was I?

# Know Who You Are

One day my son and I lay across the bed watching television and he asked me, "Dad, why are you always tapping?" I was a little dumbfounded because I didn't know what he was talking about. But not long after I blew off his question, I found myself tapping a rhythmic beat on a magazine with an ink pen. It was subconscious. There was no music playing, I wasn't thinking about music and I didn't know where it came from.

The next day at work, I asked a co-worker if she ever heard me tapping and if so did it bother her. She said, "Yeah, I have noticed that you tap from time-to-time, but I thought it was just stress-related."

That blew me away because here was something that everybody seemed to notice about me that I didn't until someone mentioned it. So I tried to stop myself from doing it over the next several days. Oh how frustrating that was!

What happened is I learned something about myself, a habit, whether stress-related or not, that drew attention to me from those around me. I did wonder if it was stress-related or some other reason so I began to monitor it for a couple weeks. I discovered that I did it at several different times—when I was frustrated, thinking or wasting time. If I made a phone call and was waiting for someone to answer, I'd tap. If I couldn't remember what my wife needed me to bring home, I'd tap. If my wife changed her mind several times about what she wanted me to bring home, I'd tap.

Now, I'm tapping about who I am in Christ. Yes, I was a bit frustrated. I was thinking about how far I'd come and how far I still had to go. And yes, I was waiting for God to answer several calls I placed to Him (I guess it was payback because I delayed when He called me).

Sometimes we ignore God when He's talking to us and then we get an attitude when we try to hear from Him for something specific and it appears that He's delaying His answer or He just doesn't hear us. In actuality, He already addressed that issue when we had the headphones on and the music blasting. That was the time He told us to listen intently.

God has equipped each of us with what we need to go into battle and to bring Him glory. We need to tap into the depths of ourselves and pull out the deposit that God placed in us. When He blew that precious breath of life in us, He crafted us to be unique yet like Him in many ways.

We are vessels to be used by God. We are beautifully and wondrously made. We are temples of the Holy Ghost. That's not a bad start.

From there, we can begin to learn and develop the unique people we are. God has given each of us characteristics that separate each of us from the next person. You might be an extrovert. I might be an introvert. You might like to run. Your neighbor might like to walk. You might kill your enemy with kindness. Your friend might do it with fire and brimstone. But like a team, each player must know his or her role and allow the coach to put you in the game at the right time to capitalize on your strengths. If God didn't gift you to speak to thousands in a coliseum, He probably won't have you speak at a rally in the nation's capital. But He might have anointed you to coordinate the event and make sure that all the "Is" are dotted and the "Ts" are crossed. That doesn't mean that God can't equip you to do something, but that might not be a strength in this particular battle.

For example, if you don't have the calling, anointing or gifting for deliverance ministry, you're the wrong person to be sent into battle in the demonic realm. It takes a warrior God trained specifically for that. I discovered that firsthand. You'll read about that in a later chapter. But what I learned at that time was deliverance ministry wasn't for me.

Part of knowing who you are is learning your strengths. The

other part is knowing your weaknesses. When you know your strengths, you can concentrate on them to exploit your enemy's weaknesses. However, if you have weaknesses and the enemy knows that, he will try to exploit them. So you have to prepare to defend yourself from the enemy's attack on your weaknesses.

That's how the enemy often gets the saints to stumble. He plays on our weaknesses by allowing us some advantage and gets us to lose sight of our weaknesses. The minute we do that, he attacks and before we discover what happened, we've already hit the ground.

Some of us talk too much. It might be a good idea to shut up for a while. Other people might trust the wrong people. Maybe we need to sharpen our discernment. Some people put too much confidence in themselves and get blindsided by the enemy. Me? I'm too loving. I feel that I can love the hell out of somebody. Damsel in distress only played into my need to be needed.

One of the things that I've learned to do is to first realize that I can do nothing without God. I look at myself and ask myself, "Where would I be without God?" The second thing I do is maintain my strengths. If I am good at quoting scriptures in a time of temptation, I try to memorize a scripture that would cover me in different situations. Or if I have the gift of exhortation or encouragement, I learn new ways of doing so. I also look for ways to develop the weak areas. You might have to experiment to see in what areas you are skilled. When I was in college, I thought I would be excellent at playing the alto saxophone (in part because I thought I looked cool with one). But if I had to play a famous jazz song to get my degree, I might be a part of the 20-year graduation plan. It wasn't until I tried it that I realized a simple fact – if I was going to be a saxophonist, I had a lot of work to do.

With that said, I learned another strategy in basketball that I translated to this spiritual battle. Not long after I started playing basketball, opponents would try to defend me to the left side because I was better at going to the right. Until I worked on developing my left hand dribble to mirror the skill level of my right hand, I gave the appearance that they were equally strong. I would dribble the ball up the court with my left hand while there was no defensive pressure. When I got close enough to the basket, I switched to my right and drove to the basket before the defender could realize that I didn't have a very strong left hand. All the while, I was developing strength in the left hand. One of my strengths became having the ability to go either left or right. But it took work and a strategy.

Similarly, I learned not to divulge my weakness. The enemy already tries to figure out what he can do to defeat you. The last thing you want to do is help him. Christians don't realize sometimes they set themselves up for a fall by speaking their weaknesses and confessing that they have no control when it comes to that particular weakness. For example, if you know that alcohol is a nemesis and a pawn used by the enemy to get you to lose control and get into fights, don't say, "If I get one drink up in me, I would do anything." The next thing you know, an old (so-called) friend pops up out of nowhere with the drink you used to spend quality time with. The next morning you wake up in jail with bumps and bruises, wondering how you got there, whom you'd been fighting and who has something to make that headache go away.

The Bible tells us in Proverbs that life and death are in the power of the tongue. If you are going to speak some things, speak life.

Confession is good for the soul, but stupidity leads to many uncomfortable consequences. Identify the areas of weakness to develop them, not to tear yourself down. Your goal is to know yourself and be the best you that you can be. This is a time that you really should desire to be all that you can be... in God's army.

# The Devil Wants You or What You Have

The devil wants you, your family and what you have. When I took a hit for the kingdom's sake, the devil's attack was not just about me. The devil wants me to serve his cause. He wants my family because it is so blessed and anointed. He really wants what we have, favor in God's eyes and to be called a child of the King. But the devil's fate has been sealed a long time ago. So he just wants to wreak havoc on the saints of God so that we would feel miserable the way he and his servants do.

When I counseled this devil, it was no different. Now that the blinders of deception are off, it's very clear now.

The devil knew his fate for committing the "unpardonable sin" – blaspheming the Holy Spirit. Blasphemy is expressing disrespect for God or something sacred. It is the defamation of the name of God. The Catholic Encyclopedia says blasphemy is gross irreverence towards any person or thing worthy of exalted esteem.

Hopelessness was one of the primary reasons that the devil sought to kill, steal and destroy.

That's why I said counseling the devil almost cost me my life.

The devil doesn't fight fair and wants to kill those who put their trust in God. The devil wanted attention from the church and its leadership. The devil wanted to steal me from my wife. He wanted my family. He saw in my family what he always dreamed of and he wanted a part of it. He wanted my in-laws. He was jealous of Tammie, the beautiful, prophet of God, who was respected in the church, loved in the community and was a good mother and wife.

He wanted to steal members of the church, one by one. His plan is to pick us off one at a time or all at once. It doesn't matter to him. In a later chapter, I'll share more about who the devil is, his strengths and weaknesses and his ultimate purpose as it relates to you and me. But I want to briefly share a glimpse of the enemy's desire to have you, me and what we have.

The devil knows who you are. He knows you have the favor of God. He knows that you are destined for greatness. Who wouldn't want those things? Add the fact that you have a beautiful wife or handsome husband, you become even more desirable. In many cases, he is not permitted by God to kill you or have what you have so he attempts to make your life the living hell in which he exists.

Take Job, for example, the Bible says that Satan was in heaven meeting with God and the angels and God permitted the devil to take Job through some trials and tribulations. God said that whatever he does, the enemy could not take Job's life. But life as Job knew it died as the enemy turned up the heat. The devil was jealous that Job was so blessed. He even had to endure his wife telling him to curse God and die and his friends bailing on him. In the end, we know that Job received double everything he lost because he remained steadfast and didn't let the enemy's attack destroy him. He had to endure through the attempts.

# Know Your Enemy

It's important that we learn what we're up against when we go to battle. Earlier, I used the analogy of being in the war room with God devising a plan to help you in your current situation. In the war room, we learn our strengths and weaknesses—how to maximize the strengths and how to guard against the weaknesses being exploited. That's a part of knowing yourself.

Equally important is knowing your enemy, your opponent in the battle. During a message I preached years ago, I likened it to a boxing match in which the boxers learn everything they can about their opponents before they step into the ring. Boxers go as far as bringing in sparring partners with similar fighting styles to gauge their potential success both offensively and defensively. It requires watching film of their opponents, reading about their strengths and weaknesses, and also learning about their driving motivation for being in the ring at all.

Why is all of this important? It's simple. You wouldn't approach a boxing match with Prince the same way you would one with Mike Tyson. You'd have to decide whether you're going to be the aggressor or if you will be a counter-puncher. Will you brawl or dance around the ring to avoid a big punch from the likes of a hard-hitter like Mike Tyson?

Well, the devil is our enemy. His mission is to steal, kill and destroy, by any means necessary. We spend a lot of time learning about God, which is great. But we forget to prepare ourselves for the one we're going up against. It's a big mistake to overlook our opponent. We usually wait until we've been tripped and entangled in the enemy's web of confusion before we start identifying where and how he deceived us. Hopefully, this chapter will shed some light on the darkness and you will be able to avoid the attack and if you can't avoid it, at least you can be ready, willing, and able to overcome it. I learned some things in the war room in preparation for possible attacks, but I know the enemy better after being sucker-punched by him. I hope this helps you bob and weave to escape a punch by the devil and that will allow you to throw a knockout punch of your own.

## Who is the devil?

The devil is a fallen angel that by definition means slanderer, accuser, and adversary. He was originally holy, the angel of light called Lucifer. He also was described as being beautiful, intelligent and powerful and had the assignment, among other things, to stand in the presence of God. Most people have heard that he was the chief musician.

There are several passages of scripture that define Satan.

Ezekiel 28 describes Satan. Jesus tells the disciples in Luke 10:18 that he saw Satan fall from heaven like lightning. Isaiah 14:12-15 gives this account:

> *"How you have fallen from heaven, O morning star, son of the dawn! You who once laid low the nations! You said in your heart, 'I will ascend to heaven; I will raise my throne above the stars of God; I will sit enthroned on the mount of assembly, on the utmost heights of the sacred mountain. I will ascend above the top of the clouds; I will make myself like the Most High.' But you are brought down to the grave, to the depths of the pit."*

Because of his pride, Lucifer was kicked out of heaven and sentenced to eternal life in hell. But first he had a stop on earth and that's where we come in. We are faced with dealing with an adversary that still wants to be God and because of his battle with God, we are pawns that the devil wants to use in an attempt to beat God. The sad part of it is that the devil knows just like the rest of us that he is already defeated and his fate is sealed. Those who overcome the enemy's attack and stay on God's side can be confident that their destinies are sealed.

The devil's motivation is hatred. As I said, his goal is to steal, kill, and destroy. (John 10:10) He will stop at nothing or no one to have the temporary feeling of victory. Notice I said temporary.

Because the Scriptures tell us that if we confess our sins, God is faithful and just to forgive us and start us all over again. Satan had a fall from which he'll never recover. He wants us to think that we can't regain our footing after we've slipped. But he's a liar and he's trying to trick us. Don't be deceived.

## His attempts

The devil has many objectives and strategies he employs to try to steer us off course. Oftentimes he tries to lead us into temptation or sin. He tries to play tricks with our minds. He tries to use demonic attacks to beat and batter us into submission. He tries to trick and deceive us into believing lies about God, about ourselves and about the people that God put around us to build us up. He also tries to destroy the believers so that nonbelievers and "on-the-fence" Christians will begin to doubt their faith and eventually fall from the grace of God. But remember that God said He would not be mocked. So, as much as the devil wants to smear God's reputation by attacking one of the saints, it's just a temporary setback, not a defeat.

## His strengths

The devil knows God, believes in God and knows the Word of God. We must never underestimate his power because he is capable of killing, stealing and destroying.

He often is called the father of lies, meaning that he is the originator and is obviously pretty good at it. Through lies he has convinced many people, including some that we never would imagine, to serve him instead of God.

Do you know someone who told a lie for so long, they started to believe it? Well, the devil tries to tell us lies for so long that he hopes we believe it. He hopes that we start telling the same lie.

He also has the ability to gather wayward souls and cause them to assist him with his mission. The devil employs demons, which come in clusters, to work on Christians. When one leaves, the Bible says, it tries to come back with seven more like it.

And finally, one of his strengths is that he has an all-out assault on the Body of Christ. He doesn't take breaks or give Christians a rest, though sometimes it may seem like we're Satan-free. He's always on the attack or lurking behind a bush, in a closet, at the grocery store or even in your house.

## His weaknesses

The devil's biggest weakness is that he is not God! He found that out when he was evicted from heaven and God sealed his fate. That only should assure us that we have the upper hand.

But we can't get complacent because the devil will continue to pound us until he convinces some into thinking he's won. As I said earlier, the devil will not stop just because you had a good time at church, choir rehearsal, or whatever.

The enemy can't stand at the name of Jesus. Every knee must bow at that name, demons flee at that name and there is all power in that name. Likewise, the Bible says that without the shedding of blood, there is no removal of sin. So as Christians, the blood of Jesus still has power over the enemy and all of his antics. We must be careful not to diminish that power with faithlessness, but plead the blood with power and authority.

Since the devil knows his fate, he tries to deceive us like he deceives himself. We need to remind him of the Scriptures that give us assurance that our God reigns and that we have a reward in heaven if we don't faint or give into the enemy's lies.

## The Devil's Past

When Satan was cast out of heaven, he came here with baggage. He brought with him the pride that caused him to think that he could be God and do God's job better than Him. All of the issues that he didn't want to deal with, he brought with him.

His pride was the primary reason for his downfall and as he

plummeted, more of his true character came out. In life, we are faced with trials and tribulations that will help determine whether we are strong or weak. If we endure one trial, we find out that we can overcome the enemy's attack. But if we fall short during another trial, we discover that there are areas that we need to strengthen or the enemy will exploit us again. It's swim or sink. Kill or be killed. Through it you define your character and when you reach a certain place in your life you will have accumulated baggage along the way to go with the strengths gained through the process.

However, there was no good the devil brought with him. There are no silver linings in his mission.

## The Devil's Present

No matter how many times we remind the devil of his past and inform him about his future, he seems to always feel like he has the victory.

When a saint stumbles or succumbs to one of the enemy's tricks, the enemy rejoices with the false hope of achieving one of the points of his mission. But he seems to forget that God is the redeemer of man. The minute that a man repents of his sins, the Bible tells us God forgives him. Although others may hold the actions against him or her forever, he or she has a clean slate with

God.

The devil, on the other hand isn't as fortunate. His current state looks like his past. And that looks like his future. So no matter how our situation looks at that present time, the devil's situation is bleaker.

Well, the devil that I counseled was all for revealing its past, using it to lure me in. How could someone as caring and loving as I hear such tragedy and not want to help? The stories began at four years old, first being molested. They continued with rape, pregnancies, miscarried children, sacrificed children, other children being kidnapped from nearby states and nights of sexual exploits by mothers, fathers, siblings and friends of the family, and even cannibalism. Like the devil we read about in the Bible, this one's life was revealed in writing as well, through journals, and shared with oral histories with as much impact as African folklore.

One email detailed attempted suicides, memories of seven murdered children, and thoughts of murdering others. Other emails shared desires to flee the past, fly away like butterflies. There were hopes of having a family described there and even hope of having a true love that would make the past a distant memory. But the true spirit of the devil comes forth through lies and manipulation. We can trace the truth back to the devil's past.

Although the devil's portrayal of a loving soul appears legitimate, we learn from the past so that we don't have a repeat of history in the future.

But unfortunately, I became a part of that past. I was engulfed in a world of witchcraft and rebellion that I didn't understand at the time. I started out believing that I was doing something right. I felt good about it. I knew that at the end of this journey we both would be better people. I eventually found out that I was not only defeating the purpose I was trying to accomplish, but I was creating more problems for everybody. I was hoodwinked and bamboozled. But I allowed myself to be there. I enjoyed it. I found myself in places with someone I had no business with doing things we had no business doing. Just like other times I found myself in sin, I justified everything I was thinking and doing. We agreed that we would keep everything a secret... everything from the lunches to the phone conversations and emails to the counseling sessions that eventually led to us trying hypnosis. I didn't know what I was opening myself up to. I was simply mesmerized by everything that was taking place. I knew that no one would understand and the devil made sure that's what I thought. It was a tactic that worked. I fell for it all. But when the devil doesn't get his way, he steps up his attack and tries to take us out. So I was set-up, accused of using my position as a minister to hypnotize and take advantage of a woman. I was later arrested and charged with one count of indecent assault.

My prayer is that this book and my process, not necessarily the details of everything that happened in my life, will prevent others from having this or similar battles.

## Looking for someone to use

When the devil used the past to set me up, I wondered if I was the weak link in Pittsburgh, in my family, and in Potter's House. Did the devil seek me out to use me as a pawn in this game? That concern had been an object of prayer for a while because I couldn't understand how this could happen.

I now know that the devil doesn't just look for a weak link, but also a strong link that isn't properly and sufficiently connected to other strong links.

I have learned a lot about the spirit realm since and how the enemy looks for a body to use for his glory, much like how God looks for a body to use for His glory. I could see a war being waged in the spirit and I was stuck in the middle. The devil used me to get temporary glory. Maybe at times I was weak when I was attacked. Other times I was strong yet I was deceived.

God also used me. That was part of the battle that took

place in the spirit. I believe that God knew I would be strong enough to endure everything that came with the devil's attack and still be able to stand and proclaim the love and saving grace of Jesus Christ. I wasn't sure of that initially. But that's why God is God. He knows all. He knows the beginning from the end and the end from the beginning. When I couldn't see, He gave me His eyes. When I couldn't hear, He gave me His ears.

I remember sitting in my car, praying about everything that was going on in my life. God had enlightened me on some things, including how everyone has to take a look in the mirror and be honest with themselves if they are going to bring glory to God. I anointed my head with oil and prayed that God would cover and protect my mind. I anointed my heart and asked God to cleanse my heart and make it pure. Then I touched my eyes, my ears, my nose, my mouth, and each hand. I wanted him to touch my senses. Then I touched each one of them again and asked Him to touch my inner senses. I wanted Him to touch my very soul, every part of me. Why? Because I still wanted Him to use me.

After everything that I had been through—causing my family to suffer as the devil used me, bringing shame to my spiritual family, and letting down hundreds, if not thousands, of people who were counting on me to be strong—I asked God to use me again. It was one of those prayers that come out during the pinnacle of prayer when one is in the holy of holies. You back out and ask yourself, "What just happened? Do I know what I'm getting myself into?" But after I came down, I said, "Yeah, that's what I want. I want God to use me."

The devil was aware that I was highly respected, had a decent job that kept me in the public's eye, and held other positions in the community that would create enough publicity to make people question God and God's servants, including me. The devil thought I was weak, unable to fight, unwilling to fight, and would just lie down and die.

But God knew my heart. He knew that I was strong enough to run the race until the end and turn the attention away from the devil, who sought the limelight, back to God. Yes, he also knew that because of my heart, I would hurt and I would suffer, but not unto death.

I asked God why things had to go the way that they did for Him to get the glory. He said He had a plan from the foundation of the world. As hard as it was to understand God allowing the devil to get away with some things, I still believed that ultimately God would get the glory. I had to submit and remember, *"...the testing of your faith develops perseverance. Perseverance must finish its work so that you may be mature and complete, not lacking anything."* (James 1:3-4)

God had some things He needed to work out of me and work into me so that I would be mature and complete for the next time He chose to use me. At the same time, He was helping me become stronger so that I would recognize the devil's next attempt to kill, steal, and destroy my life or the lives of those I love.

I had to serve notice to the devil that I wasn't going to lie down and die. God strengthened me to fight this battle so that He would get the glory. I'm just being used.

I saw where the enemy was trying to use others. But I deflected those attempts, maybe in part because I wanted that attention. Maybe this set-up was just what I needed to see who I really was and what I had been living. There were a lot of questions I asked myself, not realizing that although the enemy sought somebody to use, my God didn't mind it being me. See, His plan was in effect before the enemy came up with one of his own. So, as the enemy sought people to use, I believe God deflected those attempts so that He could get glory out of my life because that's what I was praying for. Where I thought I was getting glory, I was only setting myself up for a fall. The glory that was to come was based on my response to getting up.

I remember when the devil pointed out an assistant pastor as being overly friendly and desiring to hug and touch too frequently. I did everything in my power to make sure there was no problem there, including making sure the assistant pastor was aware of the devil's past. I don't know if the assistant pastor could have survived the hit that I took.

The devil identified another potential victim—the husband of one of the associate pastors. He was accused of kissing the devil on the lips and making sexual advances. Again, I made sure there was no problem there, suggesting that it was blown out of proportion. Maybe that was the case, maybe it wasn't. I just didn't want to see the husband go through any difficulties in his marriage behind allegations such as these.

The devil also sought the Bishop after he kissed one of his daughters on the cheek after praying for her on the altar. I shared that information but didn't realize then that the devil was also targeting the Bishop.

And there were other targets. But even now, looking at the situation in retrospect, I realize that the target or targets were bigger than just one person. The devil was trying to destroy many in the process. The church was a target. The community was a target. Ultimately, the Kingdom of God was the target.

I was the one he got and we were all still victims. I still would have been impacted had it been anyone else. Obviously, the individual impact would have been different on my family and me, but I would have been hurt as well.

## The Devil's Spirit

When Jesus looked Peter in the eyes and said, "Get behind me Satan!" it was the devil's spirit in Peter that the Lord was rebuking. My Bishop taught us that spirits are illegal on earth and that they need a body in order to operate here. So he looks for people to use and he looks for people to attack, as I mentioned earlier.

Such is the case with all of the spirits associated with the devil and his demons. Lying. Anger. Adultery. Lust. Deception. Murder. Haughtiness. Pride. The list is endless. As you'll see, I had to confront many of them. However, one of the devil's spirits caught me by surprise—the Jezebel spirit.

I was reading *Unmasking the Jezebel Spirit* by John Paul Jackson and I found so many eye openers, including how the Jezebel spirit could be prevalent in men. I learned about how the devil uses the Jezebel spirit to attack men of God, the prophets and the promises of God. Many times people operating under a Jezebel spirit don't even know that's what they're doing.

> "You can usually track how Godly men or women form soul-tying relationships with an individual who operates with a Jezebel spirit. It begins in the realm of the soul. Both men and women will find emotional needs seemingly being met by this person. *For a male leader, this will often translate into sexual needs and desires. The season of seduction may eventually climax in the act of physical adultery. Thus, their ability to keep a covenant is breached. Their influence and authority is forfeited; their ministry is destroyed and God's Kingdom suffers great loss."* (pp. 37-38)

The scripture reference the book uses in this section is Proverbs 7:21-23 which says, "*With persuasive words she led him astray; she seduced him with her smooth talk. All at once he followed her like an ox going to the slaughter, like a deer steeping into a noose till an arrow pierces his liver, like a bird darting into a snare, little knowing it will cost him his life.*"

The book shed light on a lot of issues that I had been dealing with. It was a spirit that I had heard about and had some understanding about but I didn't know how it applied to my life, or how it operated in my life, or how it cost me my life. The book went further to say:

> "A Jezebel spirit will influence a woman to criticize and belittle her husband, telling him he's not spiritual enough,

bold enough, making enough money, or that he's holding her back from the ministry God has awaiting her. She may apply subtle, manipulative pressure on him by simply sighing and commenting how nice it would be to have this or that, knowing they can't afford it. She may also imply that if he really loved her, he would work harder to provide for all her needs and desires. *Such manipulative ploys put incredible pressure on a man and increase his resentment. It may also cause him to flee into the arms of another woman who is more sensitive to his needs and who makes him feel appreciated and successful as a husband." (p. 74)*

## The Devil's Future

One thing is clear. Despite his temporary victories and the black eyes that the people of God suffer, we can return to our maker and get a fresh start. The swelling from the beating that we take goes down. Our natural skin color returns and we once again can look victorious. God can breathe life into our natural and physical lives because He is faithful and He is a promise keeper even when we're promise breakers.

In contrast, the devil is defeated. That's present tense for "to be". Perpetually, the devil is defeated. We have to live with the assurance that no matter how long it takes, we have the victory in Christ Jesus. The devil has to live with the fact that no matter what he does, no matter how long he tortures us, no matter what lies he gets us to believe for a season, ultimately he is defeated. That should be comfort to those who call themselves Christians.

Those who submit to the devil's invitation to join his mission and who have decided to keep the evil spirits that he uses in them, are assured of the same fate. Death. First, a physical death and later an eternal death in hell. That's the Word of God.

# The Devil in the Mirror

What's frightening, sometimes, is that when we take a long hard look at the enemy, we realize that there are some things about him that we can say about ourselves. If we take a long hard look in the mirror, we'd see some things that God wants to evict from us, His temple and His piece of heaven on earth.

As a young man, I remember adults saying it takes a man to admit he is wrong or say he's sorry. What they were trying to emphasize was that no matter what happens, you have to look at yourself, what role you played and how you could have handled a situation differently. Jesus says it like this, in Matthew 7:3-5, *"Why do you look at the speck of sawdust in your brother's eye and pay no attention to the plank in your own eye? How can you say to your brother, 'Let me take the speck out of your eye,' when all the time there is a plank in your own eye? You hypocrite, first take the plank out of your eye, and then you will see clearly to remove the speck from your brother's eye."*

In other words, let a man examine himself.

We know that if someone else stood toe-to-toe with us and called us a devil, one of us would leave with a black eye. It wouldn't matter whether what they said was true or not. We don't like to accept the fact that we are less than what we portray ourselves to be. That's why there is a challenge to you today to take an honest look at yourself and see what's there. I wouldn't venture out and call everybody a devil, but I guarantee that you'll find some areas of yourself that God needs you to address.

I had to take that journey down the long hall to get to the mirror. Actually, I took it several times. Have you ever looked in the mirror and said, "I don't look like myself?" I did that. My eyes didn't look the same. The shape of my head seemed different. Every feature looked a bit off. I wasn't looking deep into myself; I was looking on the surface and wasn't pleased with what I was seeing. The next time I looked into the mirror, I remember asking God, "Are you pleased with me?" I hesitated in asking that question because I really didn't want to hear Him say, "No." But I knew that *I* wasn't totally pleased with me, either. God said that I was heading in the right direction.

One of the more recent times I looked into the mirror, I didn't ask God anything. I had grown and understood that there were areas of my life that resembled my God's adversary. Rather than resembling Christ, I looked more like the devil than I wanted to admit. The ironic thing about it was that others had seen it before I did. They just didn't tell me until I had taken the biggest hit of my life. The devil hit me so hard, I began to look like him. I remember we used to joke about people being hit with an ugly stick. But looking like the devil is no laughing matter.

That's a scary thought when all our lives we've seen images of Halloween devils, evil ghosts and goblins. As far as I remember, none of them was what I called attractive.

From the time I was a little boy, my mother called me handsome. If she saw me then, she might have called me handsome to soften the blow, but she would have seen the devil that I saw in the mirror.

At this point in my life, I had known God and walked closely with him for years. I had completed Christian education through the local church's school of ministry and graduated from the Pittsburgh Theological Seminary with a Certificate of Christian Leadership. I preached, taught, and wrote the gospel of Jesus Christ to hundreds, if not thousands, of people. I had been promoted to the position of associate pastor in a growing ministry and given the charge to provide spiritual covering and guidance for more than 300 people. So, I knew the Word, just like the devil.

Despite having no intentions to do so, I killed, stole and destroyed. I heard a pastor talk about being tormented for years because, as a young pastor, he thought it wasn't wrong to advise a woman to have an abortion. But as he grew in the Lord, he discovered that he played a role in killing one of God's creations. It wasn't until he understood what he did, confessed his sins and counseled from that point forward in wisdom, that he began to walk in the perfect peace of God. He looked in the mirror, faced that demon and declared that he would be free from it after more than seven years.

Well, I faced that same demon. It wasn't until I came to a greater knowledge of Christ that I understood why I had been tormented by the abortions of three of my children and the role that I played in the abortions of two other children, similar to the other pastor.

A woman from the North Carolina church I was attending got my phone number from a church directory and said God led her to call me. She explained to me that she had conceived a child out of wedlock and she knew that she wasn't supposed to deliver the child. She asked me for money to help her abort the child. I knew the woman only by name and face because she used to read the announcements during Sunday morning services. I had been praying for God to use me and I thought I was being used by God to help this woman. So I gave her money to pay for the procedure.

The other time, a college woman got pregnant by her longtime boyfriend and decided she wasn't going to keep the baby. She called and arranged the procedure, but needed someone to take her to the clinic. Because I was known to be someone people could confide in, she asked me to take her. Again, believing I was doing something positive, I did.

Initially, neither of these abortions bothered me because I didn't have a clear understanding of right and wrong when it came to abortions. I have two children, Brittnie, 24, and Bradley, 22. But I should have five. For years, I hid from everybody that three of my children were aborted. For years, I was tormented because I got a revelation that these were God's creations and I (and the women involved) killed them. We were playing God.

I love children and every time I saw a baby, I perked up. I often thought what my other three children would have looked like. I would see children on the playground and say, this one would have been about that age. That one would have been about this age. I thought about the things they would have liked to do, the places they would have wanted to go and the nicknames I would have come up with for them.

I could handle most of the general thoughts of them. The challenge came at night when I struggled to sleep. I had nightmares about them. I would see anti-abortion television ads in my dreams targeting me. I would hear chants, "Murderer! Murderer! Murderer!" I heard stories about other people struggling with abortions in their past or the deaths of their children and I could relate. But no one knew how much. They just knew that I was sensitive and compassionate.

Guilt and shame enveloped me to the point of not telling anybody what had happened. For years, I kept it inside, feeling like I was doing the right thing by protecting other people from what I was experiencing. Plus, I never wanted anybody to know that I was a serial murderer and an accomplice to two others. That's how I saw it. Even though I accepted Christ into my life and asked for forgiveness for what I had done, a part of me couldn't believe that God would really forgive me or accept me. Plus, I couldn't forgive myself.

I hadn't known anything about Post Abortion Stress Syndrome (also called Post Abortion Syndrome). I was never diagnosed with the syndrome, but the more I read about it, the more I saw myself. I was gaining a better understanding of what I was experiencing. I learned that there were other men who experienced the same thing. Women weren't the only ones who had physical and emotional challenges because of abortions. I was gaining strength.

Tammie didn't know until recently. She didn't know

about the battles I fought inside. I didn't want it to be a burden to her and I didn't want her to look at me any differently. As far as she knew, the reason I wanted another child was because I wasn't involved in the prenatal stages for my daughter and son. That played a part in it, but I thought having another child would exorcise the demons that I battled.

When Tammie said that she didn't want another child, I felt like I was still being punished for my part in the abortions. I felt that the torment, the guilt and the shame would never end. I had to face it one day. I had to get that devil out of my mirror.

It addition to the killing, I realized that I had stolen the dreams of those children and everyone they were to come in contact with. I had stolen from the world a future president of the United States, a Hall of Fame basketball player, a minister to preach the Word of God. I stole from myself because three parts of me no longer exist.

Typically, when a thief steals something, he gains something he didn't have. I, on the other hand, continued to lose pieces of myself. At times, I didn't feel I had enough left in me. I lived empty for years and felt like I would eventually waste away.

I basically robbed the world of the 'me' that I could have been. The torment robbed and killed me time and time again over the years. Inevitably, God was going to get me to a place where I could gain an understanding of what took place, but I couldn't possibly be to others what I couldn't be to myself. There was a mask that appeared in public, but when the mask was removed, there appeared images that didn't resemble God or the person that people thought I was. They were far from the person I wanted to be. At times, I fooled myself. There were stretches where I would have no nightmares, nothing reminded me of the torment that I faced so often and I felt like I was becoming something special. I thought I was overcoming pain. But ultimately, reality struck and those demons returned stronger and brought some friends with them.

My friends and I use to say we sold dreams. In other words, we lied. We told people the things they wanted to hear to make them feel good. It took them from their reality and put them in a place they really wanted to go. We'd make up stories about ourselves to tell girls that we would later meet, just to see what type of reaction we'd get from them. Well, I tried them with myself, hoping to get an escape from years of death growing inside me. It was destroying me and it was destroying people close to me who expected me to help them.

I have always been the person that people came to for help. I seemed to always have my ducks in a row, so to speak. I was a good listener. I was compassionate. I didn't judge. I cared. I was helpful. A large part of me felt an obligation to help other people since I had destroyed the lives of these children. I knew that if someone really knew the things that I was dealing with, I'd want someone to listen, be compassionate, non-judgmental, caring and helpful. So I offered that to others. Unfortunately, that didn't exorcise the demons either, but it helped me discover who I was in Christ.

In that process of learning who I was in Christ, I looked at the entire person. I found many things that God was pleased with and many things that had to go—the demons.

Now I see how I got sucked into the enemy's trap. I could relate to the midnight baby cries, the unending nightmares and thoughts of what could have been. I was that someone crying out for help and nobody heard me. All of the secrets that I kept pinned inside because I didn't want someone to look at me differently, someone else shared. Although the descriptions of how babies were killed differed, there were common pain and comfort because someone finally entered forbidden zones.

One time, I remember touching an unplugged curling iron and snatching my hand back because it felt like I got burned. For a brief second, I could imagine the excruciating pain a woman must have felt to have a hot curling iron shoved into her vagina as punishment. That was just one of the stories this devil shared with me. My heart melted and I could not help but sympathize. The Jezebel spirit knew what it was doing. When I eventually took that walk to the mirror, I saw it too.

## Taking on the devil's characteristics

I already stated that the devil's mission is to steal, kill, and destroy. What better way to achieve his mission than to have you act like him? If he achieves that, he can get you to help him steal, kill, and destroy.

He is so sneaky and conniving that I found myself acting like him. I was saved, sanctified and filled with the Holy Ghost and yet I was conforming to his ways rather than achieving the will of God.

The strange thing about it is I didn't realize I was doing it until I had some distance from the devil and the situation. In the midst of the situation, I didn't see any wrong. I thought I was doing the right thing.

I told people stories about different things that were going on, dangling the bait to see who would bite. If they appear interested, I'd tell them more. I'd stop when they no longer appeared interested. I'd find someone else who would listen long enough for me to satisfy that hunger to talk. In essence, I was sharing stories that glorified the devil and forgetting about my ultimate goal to please the Lord. It was all disguised under the banner of doing this for God.

I didn't realize that by keeping most of what was going on between us, I was lying to my family. I was deceiving my wife. I was basically living a lie, a double life. I didn't even feel bad about it. I felt like what I was doing was right and that in the end, God was going to get the glory. Yet I was setting myself and my family up for the biggest hit that any of us had seen in our lives.

The devil knew it. It was all a part of the plan.

Ask your wife to help, she said. I didn't know that my wife had already said no. But because I felt that God was going to get the glory, I disregarded my wife's wisdom and warning. The devil was pitting me against my wife and my wife against me so that my attention would turn to deception.

When my wife didn't respond favorably, the devil tricked me into believing that my wife just wasn't understanding and compassionate as I and therefore I had to be there without anyone knowing. The deception seemed to escalate as time went by. I was becoming more like the devil every step of the way. I was getting deeper and deeper entrenched in this underworld.

## A Different Kind of Bondage

The writing on the wall was clear… "Welcome to Hell!" That was the first thing I noticed as Monroeville, Pennsylvania, detectives led me into the Allegheny County Jail. I was handcuffed and locked to the belt around my waist. There was a smell of sin and death that I only smelled one other time—the day I went into family court for a child support hearing. Oddly enough, family court was located in the old Allegheny County Jail.

The detectives and jail staff emptied the contents of my pockets into a plastic bag, scribbled my name and other identification information on the bag so they could begin to process me along with the other "criminals" that were brought in about the same time.

All my life I had lived to avoid jail, except to visit a relative or minister to a church member. Yet I still found myself in bondage, back in a state of captivity that rivaled BC—before Christ. This time, however, I had to wait for the process to play itself out. I had to wait to tell people that I was free. No matter what it looked like I was free because of my relationship with Jesus Christ. But none of that mattered at that point. I was just another criminal in the system. I was back where I belonged. Or at least that was how jail staff made me feel.

They threw me in a silent holding cell with three other brothers. Only the looks on our faces told the stories of our disgust and the realization that there were hundreds of other places that we would rather be. One brother looked like the police pulled him straight from his bed. He had a nappy head, his pants were wrinkled and he obviously slept in the shirt he was wearing or got roughed up prior to being thrown in the holding cell. If I had to guess, I would have said he got arrested for drugs based on the clothes he wore and the posture he had. But it wouldn't be appropriate to assume because that was my complaint with the jail staff. The other brother just sat there in jeans, a button-up shirt and a jacket. I learned later that he was arrested on a warrant for failure to return a DVD to the Carnegie Library.

Before long, that fishbowl that we occupied with three benches and a toilet in the middle of the floor got crowded. Right after they served us a bologna and cheese sandwich, two peanut butter cookies and a pint of orange drink, other brothers began to file into the cell. The quietness began to lift and so did the soothing smell of my cologne or that of one of the other brothers. Hygiene wasn't a priority for everybody who came into the cell that day.

The more brothers that entered, the more some brothers

talked. For some they needed to vent. For others they needed to appear and sound tough. Others just talked out of stupidity. Some were reunited with their boys from the corners who were also arrested that day. So they talked just like they were still out on the streets. They couldn't wait to get through processing so they could see their other crewmembers who already got processed or who were finishing up sentences from previous convictions.

"Man, I can't believe they got me for some 'ol dumb shit!" one guy said.

"Well, I'm in here over a DVD," brother Carnegie said.

His comment brought a laugh from the 14 brothers that were in the room at the time. He began to tell how he misplaced the DVD and ignored the late fee notices. He couldn't even remember what the DVD was about or whether he watched it. But he knows that it wasn't $5,000—the amount of bail that he needed to come up with to get out.

Another "gentleman" wanted to brag about being caught after robbing a bank. Before he ever spoke, the red dye on his clothes gave us an idea of what he was doing in jail. What was funny about his story was that a neighbor ratted him out to police. The man learned that police asked people at the bank if they noticed anybody or anything unusual around the time of the robbery. The woman said she saw her neighbor get in a car and saw red stuff on his clothes.

Not long after the man got home, police ambushed him, cuffed him and led him off to jail. He didn't even have a chance to change clothes or anything.

The first thing people asked him was, "Why did you rob a bank around the corner from your house?" Other people asked him about whether he had a disguise and was he scared and if he stashed any of the money. The man continued to talk about everything, detailing his every move, giving others the dos and don'ts of bank robbing. He finished his speech by saying federal prison will be a lot better than county jail or the state penitentiary.

I was sitting there wondering how I had gotten there. I admit that I found some of the guys to be funny, others obnoxious, and a few who seemed in the same state of mind that I was in. We just couldn't believe that we were there. All we wanted was to be home.

I was moved from one holding cell to another. This time I had to wait to be fingerprinted and photographed. When they called me to go here, I thought the process was winding down and I would soon make bail and be going home. A couple more hours passed in that holding cell. When I got there, another group of about a half dozen guys were there waiting to be fingerprinted and photographed. One by one, guys from the first holding cell came, waiting their turn. The stories continued.

Finally they called me to be fingerprinted and photographed. As if being handcuffed and placed in the back of a police car hadn't sealed what was happening to me, the moment that I was fingerprinted I started to feel like I was a criminal. All of the forensics programs, police and law programs that I love came to my mind. I saw how fingerprints were used to track down criminals and put them being bars for life.

I remembered LA Law, Law and Order, CSI, and other programs. When I was photographed, it pushed my mindset more toward being a prisoner than someone in spiritual warfare. I was beginning to feel like I would be there for a long time, even though I still believed that my father in-law was working on paying my bail.

In the hours spent in holding cells, I had yet to make any calls from the jail, but the detectives that arrested me allowed me to call my father in-law en route to the jail. I knew that the magistrate set bond at $50,000. But I hadn't really digested all of that until I was in one of those holding cells.

The jail staffer who took my picture had the usual jokes about my name and wanting me to talk about what I was being charged with. I guess with some of the other guys willingly talking about things they did, they figured I wanted to talk too. I kept basic, giving them what they needed and what was on the affidavit of probable cause.

Afterwards, I was moved to a third holding cell, this time waiting to see a jail nurse. This holding cell was bigger with two toilets and five benches. But it wasn't enough to hold about 35 men. Many sat on the floor, lay under the benches and edged closer to the door so they could be in line to see the nurse.

It was another four hours before I saw a nurse. I was tired of waiting to go nowhere. A couple hours later, I experienced the most humiliating thing of my life. I was forced to strip out of my clothes and ordered to stand there while a correctional officers checked under my tongue for drugs or contraband. He ordered me to lift up my testicles so he could see if I was hiding anything there. He told me to turn around, grab my butt cheeks and told me to squat to make sure I wasn't hiding anything there. I had to shower right there in the open next to several other brothers and was given the red jumpsuit that officially identified me as a Department of Corrections inmate at the Allegheny County Jail.

Eventually, I made it through that process and in the wee hours of the morning I was finally taken to a cell. A guy already there was awakened when the correctional officer opened the doors for the new guys to go in.

That's when I climbed onto the top cold steel bunk with my thin padded mattress and blanket and began to pray to God. I asked Him why I was there and what am I to get from this part of the process. God whispered to me, "This is not my consequence." That was the word I held onto for three more days until I was finally released on $10,000 bond after Del Greco won a reduction hearing. I had seen enough of the demons there. I was ready to go.

## Identifying the Demons

My first experience with the deliverance of a demon traumatized me. I was only familiar with a few minor aspects of deliverance ministry when demonic spirits overtook a little boy, probably five years old.

All I ever knew was that people were overcome by demons and people cast them out. The Bible gives us many examples of that. Sure, I had heard about other deliverances, but this was the first demonic attack, expression, and casting out that I had witnessed.

Bishop Carswell walked down the center isle of the church as he preached during a Sunday morning service. He touched the shoulders of members of the congregation as he passed them. When he reached the pew where the little boy was, he extended his hand and the little boy bit Bishop Carswell.

The boy's mother grabbed his arm and pulled him away from Bishop Carswell, trying to control the youngster. Others also grabbed the boy as he became rowdy in the middle of service. I helped restrain him as members of the ministerial staff (many with deliverance ministries) began dealing with the demons that were causing the boy's face to distort and causing him to use profanity.

We eventually took the boy to the lower auditorium because the process distracted people from hearing the word. While there, the deliverance ministers began speaking to the demons, ordering them in the name of Jesus to leave the boy. See, God gives some people a special anointing with power and authority to cast demons out of people. These ministers called the boy's demons out by name—profanity, disobedience, anger, and rebellion. They commanded each one to leave the boy and ordered them and any other associated demons not to return.

Ten minutes later, the same boy that was uncontrollable and shouting obscenities stood before the congregation proclaiming that God was good and that he was a good boy. The church of probably 300 people began to shout and praise God as the boy stood smiling, wondering what the people were so excited about.

Even though I saw God move in a miraculous way and deliver the boy that day, the experience wasn't one that I looked forward to again. Actually, I purposely kept my distance from such encounters.

Tammie, on the other hand, is an anointed prophet of God with a deliverance ministry. Movies such as "Fallen" with Denzel Washington and "The Exorcist" and books like *Pigs in the Parlor* and *Witches in the Pews* that involve the spirit realm or battling the demonic appeal to her.

To each his—or in this case her—own. It just wasn't for me.

## How to identify them

The Bible says that God's people are destroyed because of a lack of knowledge. The first thing that we need to do is read God's word. Several passages in the Bible, especially in the Gospels, deal with demons. Jesus casts them out on numerous occasions. Other passages, such as I Cor. 6:9-11, identifies some types of evil spirits that will keep people from inheriting the kingdom. Among them were: sexual immorality, idolaters, adulterers, drunks and homosexuals. Verse 11 says, "And that is what some of you were. But you were washed, you were sanctified, you were justified in the name of the Lord Jesus Christ and by the Spirit of our God."

Galatians 5:19-21 describes the deeds or works of the flesh—sexual immorality, impurity, and debauchery; idolatry and witchcraft, hatred, discord, jealousy, fits of rage; self-ambition, dissensions, factions and envy; drunkenness, orgies and the like. The second part of verse 21 says, *"...I warn you, as I did before, that those who live like this will not inherit the kingdom of God."*

It doesn't get any clearer than this. We have to learn to

identify the things that create a wedge between our inheritance and us. That's like looking into the mirror and something is standing between the mirror and us, yet the reflection that we can see doesn't appear to be what God said.

## Generational curses and blessings

Most times, we understand how our actions bring about the consequences and wrath of God. But the word of God is also clear about blessings and curses that are realized for generations.

Generational curses are judgments that are passed on to a person or persons because of sins perpetuated in a family or bloodline for generations without atonement.

The demons that we wrestle with sometimes are visited upon us because of the sins of our fathers, grandfathers and even further up the genealogical pipeline. We are able to decide whether we want to be blessed or cursed. But if we are trying to bring a halt to generational curses, we must realize the demonic attack and the strategic plan the enemy is using not just to keep one of us bound, but our entire family.

My father was returning from Germany where he attended the funeral of my half-sister's mother. He had a layover in Pittsburgh. He and I thought it would be a great idea for me to meet him at the airport and hang out for a couple hours before he boarded his connector flight to Colorado.

Well, bad weather cancelled his flight until the next morning, giving us the pleasure of having him stay at our house for the night. If that wasn't enough, it gave Tammie a chance to ask him tons of questions about why he never wanted to get married, his treatment of his current girlfriend and his experiences with women over the years.

Most of the conversation fit the mold of a Saturday Night Live skit, or one on Comedy Central. But I don't think that show or that network could have written what I was hearing. The scary thing about it was that I could identify with much of what my father was saying. For years I had vowed not to be like him because I felt that he had abandoned me. But the truth was I was more like him than I ever thought and we had similar experiences that I didn't know about because I didn't know him.

Tammie turned to me and said, "Your dad is a mess. Isn't he?" I chuckled. Behind the chuckle was the self-admission that there were some generational things that I never knew about. I was ignorant to who he was and in turn, I was ignorant to that part of who I was.

A few years later, I got an opportunity to spend a long

weekend with my father. It was a time of bonding, the first time I had gotten a chance to speak openly with him about going to jail, being set up by the devil and enduring the process of being made whole again. I was like a five-year-old kid following him around as he visited family members, friends and old hangouts. Although I was happy just being around him as father and son for the first time in my life, it seemed, there was more that God wanted to show me other than where my father grew up and where he played tennis with his boys.

God revealed to me more things about my father that I never knew, including his being arrested, his troubled childhood living in deplorable conditions in foster care and literally having to fight for his life growing up in Philadelphia and later in Baltimore. I learned some things about my paternal grandparents that helped me understand some generational curses that I had been living under.

As if that weren't enough, I discovered that my father and I had sexual relations with the same woman, a friend of my mother. I realized that we were more connected and bound by sexual spirits than I realized. We drove down a street in Baltimore and as we passed a building, I turned to him and said, "I had some memories in that building." He looked at me and said, "Me, too." He then explained that he used to have a sexual relationship with a woman that lived in the building. Initially, I just listened because I didn't think that we could have possibly been with the same woman. But as he tried to remember her name, he described her and it was as if a boulder hit me in my chest. I said her name and he said, "Yeah... That's her name."

We talked for a while about how weird it was for a father and son to be sitting in a car discussing their sexual relationship with the same woman. All in all I learned some things about my father that I didn't particularly care for, but I loved him more because of the same reasons. As for sharing a common sexual partner, I had to look at in terms of the bigger picture with generational curses and blessings.

Over the years, I learned a lot about generational curses—not so much from the Biblical standpoint, but from seeing a lot of things in my family that I didn't want to follow. I had both my children out of wedlock before I realized that that was a generational curse. But I broke the curse of males in my family not graduating high school when, in 1989, I graduated from the great Paul Lawrence Dunbar High School in Baltimore. I followed that by going to Denison University that fall to pursue my dream of becoming a lawyer. I had already surpassed most expectations. I had already broken many curses without knowing what I was doing.

Most of the males in my family succumbed to the streets and either ended up dead at an early age, on drugs or in prison. I remember how my uncle, Buzzy, used to go to jail often. It never fazed him to be in and out jail. Some of my cousins around my age fell into the same generational curses. One of them even enlisted in the military and within months of finishing his commitment ended up in prison behind drug sales. If you looked closely at my family, you would see that generations repeat cycles. Many family members live in the same neighborhoods, if not the same houses, that their parents and grandparents lived in. They don't see beyond their current situation. "This is the way that it's always been and this is the way that it's always going to be," you can read in their body language.

My mother was there too. Despite experiencing the heartaches of the ghetto and having opportunities to leave, that was "home" to her. Never mind that she had no legitimate job opportunities, her so-called friends were the ones who abandoned her whenever she needed help and even family members turned their backs on her when she cried out for assistance. In her recent memory were being arrested for drugs, murders not far from the front door, and facing evictions almost on a monthly basis. But there was something about being there that she wouldn't release or something there that wouldn't release her.

It was a demonic spirit that tried to keep her captive. It tried to kill her much like it did so many other people. There are demonic spirits that transfer from people to people, house to house, neighborhood to neighborhood in the ghetto. Poverty. Depression. Promiscuity. Addition. Self-control, or the lack of it. Murder. Lying. Stealing.

It wasn't until almost everybody my mother held dear to her began to die off that she finally decided to leave Baltimore. Her brother Buzzy died. Her cousin Buggy died. Her friend Carolyn died, to name a few. She had to decide that she wasn't going to let the generational curse kill her. Maybe the term generational curse never crossed her mind as she packed her bags and moved to Salisbury, Maryland, to stay with my brother, James. But something inside her told her she must live and she couldn't do it where she was.

When Tammie and I married in 1995, Brad was 4 years old. She and I decided that we were going to do everything we knew to make sure that the generational curses that had plagued our lives stopped before reaching our son. We began to tell him that he would not father a child before marriage. He would not be a womanizer. He would not take advantage of people because he was cute or he had things that people wanted. We wanted him to be a mirror of Christ and not reflect the actions that glorified our adversary, like we did, before we took a stand and accepted Jesus into our lives.

Atonement must be made before that generational curse is broken, even if you weren't the perpetrator of the sin. Then there must be a conscious effort to avoid that sin or the curse could reappear in future generations.

We have to take a long hard look into the mirror and see things that are there because of generational curses. Like those curses that hover above many inner city communities, we have things embedded in our lives from generations that we haven't looked at. Rebellion, the occult and witchcraft can literally come back to haunt you. Voodoo, magic and the days when people used to play with Ouija Boards can allow those spirits to linger in families for generations until repentance is made and the curse is broken.

Maybe your great, great grandfather had a murderous spirit and repentance was never made. That same spirit can be revisited in you or your children or grandchildren. It would behoove us to look deep into our lineage to see what could have been passed on to us without our knowledge. Repent for your sake and for generations to follow you. I had to.

It has not always been easy, especially when it comes to trying to teach what you have learned and are learning. For example, Brad is a strikingly handsome fellow with a charming personality, a combination of his parents. When he was a 15-year-old ninth grader, he learned of his charm. It reminded me of conversations I had with my mother about whether I was conceited or confident. It's the same conversation I heard from my brother as well. I wouldn't be surprised if my father and his dad had the conversations as well. For that matter, my mother probably had that conversation with her mother, seeing that she often asked me where I thought I got my good looks from.

Tammie and I still speak into Brad that he will not have children out of wedlock. We've been open and honest with him about our mistake with the hope that he will not follow those paths, but will head down the straight and narrow that we're directing him. He's on his own now at 21 and doing well.

Likewise, Tammie and I have tried to present generational blessings to Brad and I try to do the same with Brittnie, who learned of another generational curse when she had my grandson, Kyan, out of wedlock.

The Bible says that God has set before us blessings and curses and we can decide which we want.

Deuteronomy 11:26-28 says:

*"See, I am setting before you today a blessing and a curse—the blessing if you obey the commands of the Lord your God that I am giving you today; the curse if you disobey the commands of the Lord your God and turn from the way that I command you today by following other gods, which you have not known."*

That doesn't sound like a difficult decision to make. However, we often find ourselves trying to climb out of the pit of generational curses. If we choose generational blessings, we can reap the benefits of the foundation that others set before us.

Why have the sins of the forefathers revisited on us when we can have the fruit of the Promised Land? My son told me once that he will be a better father than I am, just like I said about my father. I said, "Good. I wouldn't expect anything less." I wasn't admitting that I was a bad father. I was simply acknowledging that I hoped I was laying a good foundation in which he could build upon. I hope I am setting a bar that one day he will raise. I want him to be able to tell stories of blessings that have been passed along to him.

When the time comes, Brad and Britt will get an inheritance from their father that also will be a part of the generational blessings. Most importantly, the saving grace and the knowledge of Christ have been passed down to them.

The Bible shows us that many people identified the demons that had been controlling them and received deliverance through Jesus Christ and through the Holy Spirit. That's where we can concentrate in our process. It shows us how to access the blessings as well as halt the generational curses.

Beyond the Bible, there are a number of resources to help us gain a solid foundation in identifying demons and eventually defeating them. Christian bookstores carry titles like *Pigs in the Parlor* and other resources to help you in this area. Many ministries now also concentrate on deliverance so it wouldn't be a bad idea to contact a few local deliverance ministries for direction. It could save your life and the future of your family.

## Deciding to Deal with the Demons

I had come to the end of a road. I was faced with dealing with the demons that had cost me everything that I held dear. Demons shattered my family. I had to look into my son's eyes and tell him that I wasn't the man that I was training him to be. Every morning before I dropped him off for school we would pray and I would tell him, "Represent!" He learned that I meant represent Christ, his family and the standards we set, all in excellence.

To a boy who thought the world of his dad, even to the point of thinking I could make traffic lights change when I approached an intersection, he couldn't understand how I could say I didn't represent.

Tammie didn't believe that I could say that I loved her and yet put myself in compromising situations with other women. She felt like I was living a double life. She questioned everything I had ever said or done. There was no way I could say that I loved them, she said. She even burned our wedding invitation, threw it at me and said, "This is what you did to our family." She said she hated me and asked me how it felt to love someone who hates you.

When I looked into the eyes of the girls on my high school

basketball team, it was just as painful as telling my son. I called these girls my daughters and I had let them down the same. Not only that, but they had to endure people asking them if I had done anything to them. That hurt me as well. But it was a reality that came along with the territory. When you are accused of one thing, people assume there are more things you've done. People at the school, including administrators and parents, wondered if anything inappropriate happened with students or teachers. I was even told by one administrator that they were waiting for a wave of people to come forward accusing me of things. At the church, I was even asked in an accusatory way how many others I had been in contact with in an intimate way. My co-workers at work told me they were questioned about my activities there. It was a difficult time for everybody, especially me.

A year earlier, I told my daughter she needs to make better decisions because what she does can have an impact on her for the rest of her life and cause ripple effects for those around her. Shoplifting, if it isn't dealt with, could lead to more serious crimes and ultimately lead to spending a lot of time in jail, if not ending up dead. I had to eat my own words when I talked to her after my fall. Well, I didn't deal with the demons that I knew about from my past and allowed myself to be overtaken and it cost me my family. People thought they knew some things but they had no idea.

Nevertheless, my church family discarded me. I no longer held the pastor position that helped define the good that God deposited in me. The friends I thought I had were gone. I was faced with losing my job. Legal action was pending. Finances suffered. I didn't have my family. The world as I knew it was no more.

I was alone and lonely, weak and horny, damaged and destructive. I was looking for something to attach myself to; something to give me a sense of value and worth again. I've never been a drinker, yet I found myself sitting in the bar wanting a drink. I was hoping for someone to say the wrong thing to me to give me a reason to fight. I had so much anger built up inside of me. I could see myself releasing it in a barroom brawl. I didn't care about the pain I could suffer because I didn't think I could feel any worse. I remember buying a drink and sitting it in front of me on the bar. I stared at it for about an hour. I walked out of the bar without taking a drink or a life. I guess no one wanted to fight a defeated man. The saying, "There's nothing more dangerous than a man who has nothing to lose," must have been evident that night.

What was ironic was that I never succumbed to the lure of drugs and alcohol while I was depressed. But somehow rumors circulated that I looked bad and I must have been on drugs. I was asked about it by people I thought knew me better than that. I was even asked for drugs and to sell drugs as a way to generate some income. My life was in such a whirlwind that I couldn't understand what was happening to me. I wondered if I should accept some of the offers that were coming my way.

The offer that baffles me still to this day came one day I met a woman who knew that I was a photography hobbyist. She asked me if I would take some pictures of her. I gladly said yes. I thought it would be a great way to express my creativity, release my mind from all of the turmoil that swirled around and interact with someone about something other than my depressing matters. It was a bonus that she was attractive. We scheduled to meet at a park. I arrived with my camera and ideas to produce some gorgeous images. But when I arrived, she told me that what she really wanted was to have sex with me and that she would pay me. I was shocked, yet intrigued. According to her, I knew what she was offering from the beginning. She went as far as saying that she had two other friends that would pay me to sleep with them. I was conflicted because I was separated from my wife, I was lonely, horny, and looking for something and maybe this was it, I thought. We sat in the car. She smelled good, looked good, and everything she said sounded like music to my ears. I threw my head back against the seat and closed my eyes. Her hand went from my face to my chest, down my stomach and right down my pants. So much of me wanted to have sex with her and later her friends. My mind began to justify it. "I could use the money. I could use the affection. I could use the release." But I caught myself. I told her I couldn't go through with it. She got out of the car and left. I sat there for about an hour wondering if it was ever going to get any better.

Later that night, I went to the grocery store and a 65-year-old woman with money asked me out on a date. After leaving the park, I just wanted to go home and not be bothered with anyone because I knew that I was in such a fragile place. She gave me her phone number and said call her if I changed my mind. Another woman called me and said, "If (Tammie) doesn't want you, I'll take you in a heartbeat."

That night I spoke with my mother in-law about what happened and she said she could see all of it happening. She warned me to be careful. I remember her words like she just said them. She said, "Don't be surprised by the women that will approach you. Some of them might be tricks of the enemy trying to seduce you but some of them see who you really are. You are what every woman desires."

At that moment, I had a choice. I could quit or I could deal with the demons and let God get the glory out of my life. I chose the latter. I knew that there was something inside of me that wanted to live and to prosper.

By that point, I had gotten beyond the thought of suicide. See, there was a brief moment maybe a year or two earlier when the enemy got a hold of me and almost convinced me that I wasn't who I thought I was in God. I was faced with a decision then and it crossed my mind to take my life and make everything easier for those I left behind. But I began to pray and God confirmed that He loved me and that I belonged to Him. He instructed me that there is much work for me to do and that there are people he's placed on earth to bless me and people waiting for me to bless them. He showed me Tammie, Britt, and Brad. They needed me.

From that day, I decided to press on. I wasn't sure if I would go back to Baltimore where my family is. I know they would have been hurt and disappointed, but they would have loved me anyway. I thought for a minute, my being in another city would help the healing process for everyone, including me. I thought maybe I could move to Colorado and finally be with my dad. But none of those options was the will of God for anybody at that time.

So when I was faced with these new demons, I looked in the

mirror and was petrified by what I saw. But I was ready to go to war.

I wasn't sure what I was supposed to do other than pray and read the Bible. I couldn't go to the people I normally would go to because I hurt them. Guilt, sorrow, and shame prevented me from reaching out to some people. Others withdrew from me before I could extend my hand to seek their help. The enemy wanted me isolated, hoping I would revert to a suicidal mindset. Not so!

My mother-in-law and father-in-law embraced me and assured me that they knew that I am a man of God. They knew that I let my guard down and the enemy exploited my weaknesses, but they didn't turn their backs on me. They prayed for me and encouraged me that God would work everything out. I knew that after my time alone with God, I could share with someone what he was doing and saying.

That was a testimony in and of itself. Even though I hurt their daughter and the family, they took me into their home. I was separated from my wife, yet I was living with her parents in the same house that she grew up in. That made my decision to deal with the demons in my life that much easier.

I saw that as a positive step. It wasn't easy, as their

frustration and disappointed surfaced from time to time, but it was a step in the right direction.

New Jersey Pastor Mike Hayes once said, “It takes a lot of little things to make a great thing.” He shared a story about how the bridge was built over Niagara Falls. It all started with an idea by one engineer and a kid with a kite. The engineer sponsored a contest and offered 25 cents to the first person who flew a kite over Niagara Falls to the other side. Engineers used the concept from the successful kite flight to develop plans for a bridge, including the height it would need to be, the angle of the bridge’s route, and how to anchor it. Not many years later, the bridge was erected. But it all started with a little boy and a kite.

# Defeating the Enemy

We've identified our strengths and weaknesses and have prepared ourselves for battle. We have learned some of the enemy's strengths and weaknesses and are now ready to face him. We've decided to go to battle.

Utilize your strengths and attack his weaknesses. We can begin to devise our game plan to defeat him (with God's help of course). I go back to the message that I preached where God gave me the analogy of boxing. God illuminated Matthew 4, when the Spirit led Jesus into the wilderness and the enemy tried to tempt Him. Every time the devil tried to tempt him, Jesus counter-punched him with the Word.

Matthew 4:8-10 –

*"Again, the devil took him to a very high mountain and showed him all the kingdoms of the world and their splendor. 'All this I will give you,' he said, 'if you will bow down and worship me.' Jesus said to him: 'Away from me, Satan! For it is written: 'Worship the Lord your God, and serve him only.'"*

Everything the enemy tried, Jesus reminded him that God already spoke victory and, "I'm not going to lose sight of that." Ask yourself, "What would Jesus do or say in my situation?"

Let's look at what the enemy uses in his attempts to temp Jesus.

- *If you are the Son of God, turn these stones into bread.* Satan knew that Jesus had been fasting for 40 days and 40 nights. With us, he knows when our temper is short and he sends someone to push our buttons to see if we will fly the coup. Or when you're fasting your supervisor buys donuts for everybody in your department. The enemy has studied us just like we're studying him now. It's just that no one ever told us, so we weren't aware that the fine sister that's been checking you out is just a devil in a dress with caked on make-up. The devil knows that you've been battling loneliness and fornication. Now you are the wiser because you are learning his game plan.
- *If you are the Son of God, throw yourself down and command angels to come and lift you up.* After testing Jesus in the flesh, Satan now targets His deity, His authority, His place in God as God. He was trying to get Jesus to overstep His authority and let pride overtake Him, much like what happened to Satan. If he can get our pride involved, he's won half the battle because pride goes before destruction, a

haughty spirit before a fall. That's why we often feel like we can handle things on our own. The devil is setting you up for the knockout punch. Don't fall for it or you will fall because of it.

- *You can have all the kingdoms of the world and their splendor if you bow down and worship Him.* Finally, Satan gets to his ultimate agenda... to get you to turn your back on God and worship him. Like Jesus, we need to get offended when the enemy tries to steal us away from God to serve him. The scary thing about it is that he's convinced so many people and they are usually the ones that we come in contact with every day. The people that we feel should be helping us overcome the enemy's attack have already switched sides. So we have to be careful, as my mother-in-law once told me, to watch carefully and walk cautiously.

When Jesus commanded Satan to get away from Him because the Word says to worship the Lord your God and serve Him only, the enemy left and angels came to minister to Jesus.

Jesus left that place and began to preach the word, *"Repent because the kingdom of heaven is near."* That's the same message that you're probably feeling in your spirit right now. You know, like Jesus, that victory brings about celebration. What better way to celebrate your victory than by spreading the Word?

# Spiritual Warfare: Getting the Devil out of the Mirror

Defeating the devil in general is one thing. God said that we must not conform to the world, but be transformed by the renewing of our minds (Romans 12:1-2). We learned a lot—that the battle is the Lord's, that the victory is already won, and that we are more than conquerors in Jesus Christ. We've defeated the defeatist mindset so that we can finish the race that God set before us.

There is much more required of us. We have to be active participants in this battle. One of our responsibilities is to wage war against the enemy in the spirit realm. The Bible tells us that the weapons of our warfare are not carnal, but are mighty to the pulling down of strongholds. When dealing with the enemy's attack, we have to wage spiritual warfare on a level we've never experienced before.

We've all heard of sermons about putting on the whole armor of God. Sometimes messages get so overused that we tend to ignore them because we think we've heard it all and there can't be anything new to them. But I would challenge you to listen with a keen ear whenever a preacher or teacher is ministering on the whole armor of God. It might serve as a warning that a spiritual attack is on the horizon and you need to be prepared.

But even before that happens, get it in your spirit that Ephesians 6 will help you avoid the enemy's attack, it will help you get through the enemy's attack and it will help you maintain the deliverance you receive when you get the devil out of your mirror.

Let's take a look at the armor of God:

A. **The Belt of Truth** – The devil is called, "the father of lies" so we have to have truth to combat his tricks. His antics are formulated by lies and deception. Generally, we use belts to hold our pants around our waists. If we didn't have belts, our pants would drop, exposing our private parts to the world. But God wants us to have the truth to deal with ourselves, the uncovered and covered parts. Afterward, we can turn the truth loose on the devil because we will have already learned that the truth makes one free.

B. **The Breastplate of Righteousness** – The breastplate protects your heart, your lungs, and your abdomen. What many people don't realize is that Roman breastplates also covered the back, protecting the kidneys and vital organs from getting punctured from the rear. If the enemy's fiery darts hit one of your organs, you may never recover. God wants us to guard our vital organs in battle, especially our hearts—the source of our love and compassion. It's the place where man must believe on Jesus Christ that he might become a born-again Christian.

C. **Feet Fitted with the Readiness that Comes from the Gospel of Peace** – Many theologians have debated whether God was saying be prepared to preach the Gospel of Jesus or be prepared to advocate peace, as Matthew describes in the Beatitudes, *"Blessed are the peacemakers, for they shall be called the sons of God."* (Matt.5:9) I tend to side with the latter because God gives us another weapon later. But God definitely wants us to preach the peace of God to non-believers and peace to believers in the midst of their battles.

D. **The Shield of Faith** – The Bible tells us that the shield helps us to extinguish the flaming arrows of the enemy. He could have called it the shield of truth, the shield of righteousness, or the shield of peace. It is faith that takes our belief to another level. We have to have faith to believe that no weapon formed against us will prosper. Fear and doubt cancel faith. So doesn't it make sense that faith cancels fear and doubt? When you look at the enemy in the mirror and he begins to tell you that you're the scum of the earth, hold up your shield of faith and deflect the arrows. Your faith will help you get the devil out of your mirror.

E. **The Helmet of Salvation** – The helmet protects the head. Without it, a soldier is susceptible to attacks that could take out the ability for the body to function. The enemy attempts to get us to doubt our salvation. He tries to play mind games with us, hoping that we will believe something other than what the Bible assures us is our everlasting reward for accepting Jesus Christ as our Lord and

Savior. We guard our minds by remaining steadfast in the salvation of the Lord.

F. **The Sword of the Spirit** – The sword of the spirit is the Word of God. It is our primary weapon in the battle to get the devil out of our mirrors and to keep him out. The word can be used as a defense against an attack or it can be used offensively to attack. We must know our weapon so that we can use it appropriately and wisely. *"In the beginning was the word, and the word was with God, and the word was God."* (John 1:1)

When a soldier goes into battle, he is given everything that is needed to survive. My father retired from the U.S. Army and he was proud of his service to his country. My father-in-law also served in the military, in the U.S. Marines. They both have told me about the vigorous training it takes to become a soldier. Through it you gain confidence that when conflict arises, you are properly trained and equipped to defeat the adversary.

Hopefully that is what you're getting by reading this book. Sometimes, it takes people going before us to learn the right ways and wrong ways so that we can be instructed and learn from their experiences. At some point in our lives, we've all been there. Whether we told a younger sibling not to go close to the oven when mama was cooking because they could get burned or you've told a friend about the dangers of drinking and driving. Our parents have told us not to experiment with drugs because some of them had experiences they wish they could take back.

Sometimes we listen. Sometimes we don't. When we don't listen, we eventually have to take that look in the mirror and see some things we don't like. Maybe we missed our lesson that time. But if we had heeded the message, it could have saved us years on our lives, fights with the enemy, generational curses, the loss of valuables and people dearest to you.

I'm guilty. For years, my grandmother warned me about premarital sex. My mother warned me against stealing. My aunt taught me to treat people better than they could ever treat me. My wife warned me about how friendly I am around women. Many years and lessons later, I look back on all of the mistakes that I made and the subsequent consequences and wonder what would have been, could have been had I only listened.

Had I listened to my mother's warning about stealing, maybe I wouldn't have gone to Two Guys department store that day and loaded my pockets with toys without paying. Some 20-plus years later, I wondered if my daughter's shoplifting was a generational curse? I don't know, but warfare is needed even now about stealing at Two Guys almost three decades earlier.

Looking in the mirror can be awfully painful sometimes. You begin to see things that you tried to forget, but actually they're just lying dormant until they can manifest themselves in someone you're connected to or until they rear their heads in your life again. Warfare is necessary.

It was through one of my latest lessons learned that God called me to another dimension of spiritual warfare. It was in the family room at my in-laws house during my separation from Tammie that I finally got the devil out of the mirror. A combination of factors led to my deliverance, including normal prayer and worship, spiritual warfare and deliverance. My life changed that Wednesday evening.

Many people tend to use prayer and spiritual warfare synonymously. But they are different. In its simplest form, prayer is communication with God. You talk to Him and He talks to you. Spiritual warfare incorporates prayer, but it also involves fighting the devil and his demons in the spirit realm. You are at war with your adversary as you get commands and strategies from the true Commander-in-Chief Jesus Christ.

Tammie sent me some information on deliverance that she thought would help me. Her thinking, I'm sure, was that she knew what I was dealing with and knew what I needed. I began reading the material, very curious about what it included and expecting to be enlightened. But as I started reading, my spirit perked up. I knew that I was getting into something far beyond myself. So I researched and found more material on the subject.

At that time, I was still fearful of deliverance because of the experience mentioned earlier. But there was something drawing my attention deeper into it. And for me, someone who doesn't enjoy reading much, I couldn't believe that I was engulfed in the material and it was touching every area of my life. It made me do more research. Not only was I learning definitions, I was seeing where my life came into play. Generational curses were identified. Spirits that I thought had been dealt with were present. I learned where I made some detrimental mistakes and where the enemy set me up. I learned how the enemy used my gift to love against me by sending a damsel in distress. I saw how I began to trust the devil and hid his lies, which led to me telling a lie to conceal the devil's lie. Guilt for telling a lie led to low self-esteem. Low self-esteem connects with depression. Depression says since you already sinned, it doesn't matter if you sin again. Before you know it, you're caught in the devil's trap. I was getting to the root of issues that no one was aware of but God and me.

I learned six entries of evil: willful sin, involuntary

inheritance, occult entanglement, abuse, addictions, and abandonment. I read a list of occult-related objects and activities that can lead to demonic possession, such as horoscopes, psychic healings, and necromancy.

The information was just what I needed as I had slipped into a depression that I had never experienced before. So, I began to praise and worship God in that room. My mother-in-law was at church and my father-in-law was at work. The more I praised and the more I worshipped, I felt myself getting closer and closer to the presence of God. I thanked God for speaking to my spirit and revealing to me where I was and assuring me that I wouldn't stay there.

I had known some obvious things I needed to be delivered from including anger and pride. But because I wasn't sure of what else the enemy tried to use to bring my family and me down, I began to follow the scripts in the deliverance material and called out any-and-everything that was listed until I was free. I believed that I would be a new creation when I was done.

One section listed 10 Steps to Deliverance From Satan:

- Bind Lesser Demons to Their Leader
- Work Through the System
- Ask God for Angelic Assistance

- Call Forth Undesignated Demons
- Find the Function of the Demon
- Employ the Assistance of the Victim (the person believing delivered)
- Break all Curses
- Force the Demon to Tell the Truth or Face Judgment
- Confess the Sin of Demonic Entry
- Make the Demon Pronounce His Own Doom

It takes some time and research to get a full understanding of all of this. But when you're the midst of battle, you take what you can use and use it. I followed what I could, step by step. I used the principle of binding and loosing, calling demons that I learned were linked together like loneliness and depression. I began to see which demonic spirit linked to others and that took me into warfare beyond the here and now, beyond the flesh. I began to see warfare with multiple spirits, principalities and strongholds that I was unfamiliar with. If it were a 12-round boxing match, I was prepared to go the distance. It didn't matter what stood in front of me.

I called forth angels from heaven to do battle on my behalf in the heavenlies and also right where I was in the natural. I knew God could dispatch a legion of warring angels at any time. I figured it wouldn't hurt to call in backup.

I called forth the demons I didn't know to call, seeking the demon's function and what area of my life it had been holding hostage. I was determined to win this battle.

Every time I felt a struggle as if the demon didn't want to let go or get out, I battled harder, remembering the armor of God and putting every piece into action. I realized that confession of my sins and every area of my life that allowed the demons in were bringing forth release and victory. I reminded every demon of its fate.

The warfare went something like this:

> "Satan, I rebuke you in the name of Jesus. I renounce any claims you had upon my life, in the name of Jesus. I plead the blood of Jesus against you and your demons. You have no right to this body or my mind. Any authority you thought you had is forfeited in the name of Jesus."

The material provided a list of demons that the devil uses to attack the people of God. I began running down the list asking God to help me as I rebuked the devil and each demon. The ones that I knew of were in that list. So were the ones that I didn't know. It didn't matter, I wanted to be clean and if there was anything unclean in me that night, it was being dealt with. I was binding and casting out demons like a pro. I felt my strength from God every step of the way.

> "Pride you must go, in the name of Jesus! Lust you must go, in the name of Jesus! Rebellion you must go in the name of Jesus! Witchcraft, you must go in the name of Jesus! I renounce the power of every demon associated with any of these spirits. Idolatry you must go in the name of Jesus! Addictions you must go in the name of Jesus!"

I continued until I felt totally free. Some things had no effect when I called them and renounced their power and perceived authority. But I could literally feel weight being lifted from me when I called out some of the demons such as pride, witchcraft and depression. I knew that change was taking place. Whatever was happening, I didn't want it to stop. I wanted total deliverance, total freedom and total victory over anything that kept me bound.

God showed me the séances I participated in as a kid and how the spirits lay dormant until they met up with their friends when I counseled the devil. I cast out witchcraft associated with that spirit and any like it. I saw the day I lost my virginity at 10 or

11 years old to one of my cousin's friends. She was two years older than me. Kids in the neighborhood began experimenting with sex when they were 12 and because my cousin had to take me places, I began experiences things earlier than friends my age. God showed me how it kicked off a sexual drive in me. I called out lust connected with that. I called out the anger against my father that I thought I already addressed for his not being there for me when I was younger. The anger was never dealt with so I had no choice but to deal with it.

Following the praise and worship, and warfare and deliverance, I went back to thanking and praising God. They were the first weapons leading to my freedom. I thanked Him for allowing me into his presence and for the deliverance. I thanked him for sparing my life and for sparing the lives of those around me because of the experience I shared with him that night. Because yes, I felt like I could have killed a lot of people during that time. I told God I looked forward to the rest of the work that was to come.

He reminded me of Psalm 51, a scripture that helped me not long after I had realized how badly I messed up. When I read the scripture, I remembered promising God that I would preach and teach from this experience when he brought me out, just like David did. Even through the depression, I never doubted that

God would do it. I recommitted myself to that promise that night.

Psalm 51 says:

*"Have mercy on me, O God, according to your unfailing love; blot out my transgressions. Wash away all my iniquity and cleanse me from my sin. For I know my transgressions, and my sin is always before me. Against you, you only, have I sinned and done what is evil in your sight, so that you are proved right when you speak and justified when you judge. Surely I was sinful at birth, sinful from the time my mother conceived me. Surely you desire truth in the inner parts; you teach me wisdom in the inmost place. Cleanse me with hyssop, and I will be clean; wash me, and I will be whiter than snow. Let me hear joy and gladness; let the bones you have crushed rejoice. Hide your face from my sins and blot out all my iniquity. Create in me a pure heart, O God, and renew a steadfast spirit within me. Do not cast me from your presence or take your Holy Spirit from me. Restore to me the joy of your salvation and grant me a willing spirit, to sustain me. Then I will teach transgressors your ways, and sinners will turn back to you. Save me from bloodguilt, O God, the God who saves me, and my tongue will sing of your righteousness. O Lord, open my lips, and my mouth will declare your praise. You do not delight in sacrifice, or I would bring it; you do not take*

*pleasure in burnt offerings. The sacrifices of God are a broken spirit; a broken and contrite heart, O God, you will not despise. In your good pleasure, make Zion prosper; build up the walls of Jerusalem. Then there will be righteous sacrifices, whole burnt offerings to delight you; then bulls will be offered on your altar."*

I heard other ministers preach from this passage many times. I have used it in counseling sessions to encourage believers who were struggling in various areas and needed to know that God cares and has a plan for His people to be reconciled back to Him. I used it on other occasions to share of His love, His compassion, His healing, and His deliverance. We, too, must be like David. We must confess our sins, cry out to God and assure Him that we will submit to His plan.

I wrote the following poem/psalm with that in mind. I call it, *"A Song of Repentance."*

## A Song of Repentance

*I've come to you in sadness, a bowed down head lifting my voice.*

*I beg you for forgiveness, because of another careless choice.*

*I know that you are disappointed. I know that you expected better.*

*I know that you had faith in me to keep my act together.*

*Yet I let you down, although I never really intended to.*

*I even let myself down; I wasn't the person I thought I knew.*

*But through it all I praise you, for you've cleaned me up again.*

*Even when I let you down, you still called me friend.*

*So through a repentive spirit, I acknowledge my every fault.*

*Because of your grace and your mercy, I have a brand new start.*

*Now I have a second chance to tell you what you mean to me.*

*And through my lifestyle I will strive to be who you've called me to be.*

For whatever reason, I never was able to keep a journal. Sometimes I wrote things that I never wanted to read again, let alone have someone else read. My therapist thought it was a good idea to release some of the feelings and emotions that I bottled up inside because I felt like I was alone and no one understood me or what I was dealing with. I started, but I never got beyond a page or two.

I know that journaling is great. I've recommended it to many people I've counseled and it has been a blessing to a lot of them. It just never worked for me. What did work was alternative writing—the poems, stories, letters, essays and sermons. Now it has extended to include writing for television and movies. They served the same purpose, I assume. Every time I wrote about some feeling, thought or experience, I recognized the areas that I still needed to address. It helped me wage warfare against the enemy, who continued his attack on me despite my mounting victories. When the devil thought he had me cornered, isolated and ready to surrender to his ways, God used my writings to help me overcome the attacks.

When I felt depressed and wished someone was there to tell me they understood what I was going through and that everything would be all right, I wrote about the place I was in the spirit. Through my writing, I often found myself identifying where I was and what I needed to do to overcome my current situation. Without fail, I always seemed to point myself back to God.

That's how this project began. I recommend you write as part of your process of becoming whole. Whatever you write, whether it's a journal, story, or poem, I'm sure God will bless it.

One time I felt alone and abandoned, I wrote a poem called, "On an Island." I'm sure you can relate to this poem if you've ever had to look in the mirror and deal with something other than what God created. You can remember crying your eyes dry. I cried so much one time that my face hurt. A poem couldn't quite capture exactly what I was feeling, but you might find yourself in some of my words.

## On an Island

*My tears have reached an island,*

*Silent, yet powerful*

*As it crashed upon the skin of the shore.*

*Blindfolded darkness of the sky*

*Bends in the background, touching my tears.*

*What happens to the sound when the lights go out?*

*What happens to the waves when my tears come?*

*What happens to the wind when I leave myself?*

*What happens when I don't want to be alone?*

*My tears keep me company at night,*

*Kissing my cheeks and my lips.*

*Leaves fall the same way,*

*And every once in a while someone picks one up*

*And keeps it. Sometimes.*

*I name this island with my tears.*

*First name...*

*Middle name...*

*Last name...*

*Nickname...*

*Other nicknames...*

*I begin to name every creeping thing.*

*Every crawling thing. Everything swimming in my tears.*

*Tears that remain on shore dry out,*

*Like an everlasting fossil of the mind.*

*The tide pulls back the tears,*

*Only to collect more*

*And come back, crashing to the island.*

Every time I wrote, I sent a blow to the devil and his plan. Even when I wrote about being depressed or sleepless nights that I felt like I was going to drown in my tears, deliverance was taking place. I was going from a lower state to a higher state. You might have to read some inspirational material to remind you that the victory is already yours. You might need to sing a song. On several occasions, I read this song that I wrote so that I didn't forget what God had already done.

## I Am Free

*I am free to worship, that's why I praise His holy name.*

*I am free to worship, when I dance I'm not ashamed.*

*For my God saved me, healed me and I know that He cares.*

*So I will worship God the Father anytime, anywhere.*

*I am free.*

*I am free.*

*I am free.*

*I am free.*

*You can look at me like I'm crazy, while I sing a song of praise.*

*But He's the one who broke the chains; He's the Ancient of Days.*

*He showed me love when there seemed to be no love.*

*He gave me life and changed me from everything I was.*

*I am free.*

*I am free.*

*I am free.*

*I am free.*

*I owe Him praise. I owe Him worship. I owe Him honor and glory. I owe Him me.*

*I am free.*

*I am free.*

*I am free.*

*I am free.*

*I owe Him praise. I owe Him worship. I owe Him honor and glory. I owe Him me.*

One of my next writing projects includes the screenplay and movie version of this book, which allows me to add the visual component to this next stage of this 2,000-step process. Some people receive their blessings through the written word. For others, it takes a visual presentation for them to see the story unfold. I know this is yet another part of how God plans to use my story and my experiences to help others achieve their goals.

## My Process

Everybody's process is different. Everybody's timeframe is different. What we have to remember is that it is a process that has a beginning, middle, and an ending (although I'd recommend that the ending be perpetual). What I mean by that is if you have a goal, there might be a process to reach that goal. It may have 2 steps, 5 steps, 12 steps, or the 2,000-step process we talked about earlier. But once you reach that goal, set another one and let the new process begin. We've all heard the saying… "An idle mind is the devil's workshop." We don't want to give the devil any room to use us or to allow someone to cause us to fall. The timeframe it takes going from stage to stage varies also from person to person and situation to situation.

It's best that you seek God and know where you are in your process. I will share with you another part of the process that I went through. I didn't always know where I was in the process as I was going through it. At one point, I felt like I was on an island again but this time things were going well. I simply felt that I was going to be blindsided and knocked off my feet because I didn't know where I was. I prayed to God and asked Him to identify the period in my life so that I could submit totally to His plan for my life. I needed to know for my continued development. I believe

God appreciated that I wanted to surrender my will for His.

My process (up to the time of this writing), was as follows:

- *Repentance* – This included an inexplicable amount of pain and sorrow, guilt and shame. Repentance is being sorrowful for what you did. It involves acknowledging the wrong, asking for forgiveness and turning away from the actions that put you in that place.
- *Withdrawal* – There are two types of withdrawal that I suffered. The first had to do with voluntary withdrawal where I had to pull myself away from people or things for their sake and for my sake. I cut off communication with a couple friends because I knew their families or friends wouldn't understand what I was dealing with. I call that 'cold turkey' withdrawal. The second type of withdrawal was involuntary or forced withdrawal. Yep. I call that 'hot turkey.' There have been times when I was barred from certain places because things were unresolved and it could have created more problems. One of the most painful of this type of withdrawal was when Tammie, concerned about demonic spirits that she felt had attached themselves to me, prevented me from being alone with my son. I was hot! Hence the term... 'hot turkey.' During these withdrawals, my body

and my spirit reacted and responded similar to how a drug addict acts during detoxification. I even had several hot and cold turkey withdrawals from Tammie.

- *Warfare* – I had to realize that there was a battle going on around me and that I had to get involved. I was battling myself and didn't know it. People were waging war against me and I didn't know it. I had to go to war. I also had to fight the devil. I found myself in the battle of my life and had to learn to fight differently and on the move.
- *Celebration* – When you've repented, gone through the withdrawal stage(s), and have experienced some success on the battlefield, it's only natural that you rejoice for the victories won. Sometimes the small victories are just as good celebrating as the major ones and the celebrations give you courage and strength to continue.
- *Second Dimension of Warfare* – In this dimension, you know you have to take your warfare a little higher. Maybe the enemies are a little bigger, a little craftier or a little more ruthless. This dimension doesn't come as a surprise to you because you were aware there would be more battles after your brief time of celebration.

- *Sustained Time of Celebration* – Now that you've come through the second dimension of warfare, you feel the most significant of battles are behind you. This is the place where you tend to let your guard down a bit, hoping that the status quo would be good for a while. But that time runs out before you know it when the enemy ambushes you, like he did me. He'll use the least likely people or things to attack you.
- *Third Dimension of Warfare* – The ambush pushes you into the third dimension of warfare, where your focus goes from gaining an advantage and taking hostages to annihilating your enemy. You see what his intentions are by now and you have no choice but to be on the offensive because the next ambush could end it all for you. This was one of the times I felt I could literally kill some people. I knew that some people wanted me dead.
- *Recovering What Was Lost* – At this point, you got things straight with God, you've dealt with yourself and you've dealt with your adversary. Now you can look toward restoring what was lost. Of course some things will be regained along the way. But until you go through various stages, you won't fully be able to regain or retain these things. There's a profound maturing in this process. But

don't expect everything to be restored. God meant for some things and people to be lost in the process.

- _The Great Commission_ – Jesus tells the disciples in Matt. 28:19-20 to, *"go and make disciples of all nations, baptizing them in the name of the Father and of the Son and of the Holy Spirit, and teaching them to obey everything I have commanded you. And surely I will be with you always, to the very end of the age."* Through my process I learned that God was calling me to reach more people and teach them the ways of Christ by sharing what God has done for me. That's an interesting concept when you've been in a place where your character and integrity have been tested and attacked. The same person that looked into the mirror and saw the devil is the same one that God wants to use. Yes. That was I.
- _To Be Continued..._ I'm still in the process.

## Beware the Premature Celebration

When you've gone through such an extensive and intensive process, you tend to look for places to celebrate. That's all well and good and encouraged. However, sometimes we get to a place that we feel the victory has been won and we become complacent. Before long, the devil rears his ugly head and blindsides us. There is no such thing as a vacation for the devil.

I knew my process wasn't over despite significant progress in every area of my life. I knew the enemy didn't appreciate the transformation that was taking place in my mind and the purifying going on in my heart. So, just as I looked into the devil-free mirror to explore the miraculous work that God was working on the potter's wheel, suddenly the devil reappeared.

I don't know if someone ever walked up behind you while you were looking in the mirror. No matter how attractive they are, the sudden appearance sends fright into you. Well, the devil reappeared in my mirror and it sent a shockwave through me. But here's the kicker. Throughout my process, I was ridding the enemy from my mirror and beginning to see God more in the mirror. That work was being done on me. The devil I was getting out of that mirror was the devil in me. It's a whole new battle when the devil reappears in your mirror but this time, the devil is using others to cloud the enchanting picture that you had begun to see.

For that moment, it feels like all the progress that you've made in your process has been null and void when the devil reappears. We celebrated the victory a little too long and the war was still being waged. Also, we already know that the higher we go in God, the more weight the devil will try to use to pull us back down.

I felt every pound of that weight on my shoulders and I couldn't understand how within a matter of minutes (literally) people, places and things can go from perfect to poor.

I have a friend who had experienced some difficult times in her relationship with her husband and her children. But as a couple, they decided they would do whatever it took to keep the family intact and to mend every broken area. I would be lying if I said they had done that, but they were making a concerted effort to have the marriage they were capable of having. Communication was improving. They returned to having family night and spending quality time together. They supported each other's activities whether it was sports, theater, careers, and extended family functions.

As soon as they put things on cruise control, it seemed like all hell broke loose. Well, truthfully, that's what happened. Hell broke loose on them and their worlds came crashing down. The enemy stepped in and tried to destroy everything they had worked to establish. They were staring divorce in the face. The family was being pulled apart. Everything they saw as promising and encouraging turned into a horrible domino effect that caused them both to say, "How did this happen?"

Although they both had a part to play in it, when they looked closer the devil used other people to transfer negative images into their mirrors. It all happened in one day.

The bad news is that the marriage was over before they realized how much the devil plotted this in the beginning of their process. He felt if he could get them to a certain place, he could divert the strength they gathered along the way and make them vulnerable to an ambush. My friend has decided to share her story with others to help them avoid a similar ambush in their process.

Even though I was watching carefully and walking cautiously, I couldn't stop the emotional battle that came along with the attempted attack. There were some things that I didn't look at spiritually. I knew that the enemy would throw curveballs and send people to disrupt things. And I didn't handle it properly. I felt that I had overcome so much to get to that point and shouldn't have to deal with things that I thought were behind me or battles for others. If people can't understand what took place, that's their problem, I thought.

Here's one example. Tammie and I had made significant strides in re-establishing some basic things that we lost in the midst of this process, such as communication, praying for each other and working toward common goals. Although things were going well, we were trying to be careful not to send each other mixed messages and trying not to read into things that may not have been there. But truth be told, we were enjoying the fact that God had done as much as He had in both of us that we had reached such a positive milestone. Even though we were still separated, we were enjoying each other's company, going on dates, and writing love letters. We were talking about *when* we got back together, not *if* we got back together.

What I didn't anticipate was the devil using other people to cloud our vision. Nothing had changed between us. I didn't do or say anything stupid. But because things from the past resurfaced through other people, it caused immediate distance to be thrown between Tammie and me. Maybe there were some unresolved issues that arose. Maybe fear crept in. Maybe she realized that the battle wasn't over and she wasn't ready to continue the fight. So she wanted space.

Now I had taken it personally. I couldn't understand the

need for it because we were so close to being on the same page. How could any issue push us apart again after we'd come so far? How can we not overcome any challenge? I felt that action was a signal of the end.

I began to prepare myself for the worst—life without my wife, my helpmeet, my friend, the one that God chose for me. I thought about all the times that I told Tammie that she completed me. I thought about how empty that space would be that God cut in my heart for her. I had already experienced that to a degree in that withdrawal stage but there was hope that reconciliation was still a possibility. Emotionally, I was a wreck because now it seemed that all that was left was goodbye.

I remembered something I told Tammie early on in the process: "I am going to fight for my family. I'll do whatever it takes to make things work." I meant that. But another thing I meant just as much was that I wasn't going to fight her. I'd slay dragons, fight giants and wrestle alligators. I'd put my life on the line for my marriage and my family. But I refused to go to war with her if she didn't want me.

After celebrating so high from the progress that was made, the fall back to the reality that the war rages on almost took me out. I had to recoup. I had to throw on my armor, refer back to the things that helped me grow into that celebration stage and mount a new attack on the devil.

I got two other rude awakenings dealing with my court case. The first time I got excited that my court date had finally come and I could put the entire experience in the proper folder. I could move on with my life. But I got a call from my attorney telling me that the prosecution had requested a postponement. We knew the court was going to grant it because I had requested a postponement when I switched attorneys. My life was once again put on hold until a new trial date was set.

Similarly, I celebrated the progress of my court case. My attorney, the investigator and myself were confident in the case from the beginning but that confidence grew as we found more people with pertinent information that would help us. Witnesses were prepared to testify about how the devil set me up. They included phone conversations about the planned ambush, threatening comments about trying to steal me from my wife and family, and threatening to involve the police if my job didn't fire me. There was also trickery that attempted to get me to say something out of context that would have incriminated me. These were all reasons to celebrate but when it was time to step forward, witnesses backed out, some said they didn't want to get involved now; they changed their stories and conveniently couldn't find the material that would have been key evidence at trial. I had to regroup. I felt the spirit of anger rising again. This was my life that people were toying with. I had to return to the promises that God made me and believe that no matter what happens, no matter who testifies or who doesn't, God was in control.

# Net Losses, Net Gains

## Losses

Most of the things that I lost as a result of counseling the devil and submitting to my process are measurable in the sight of others, especially the chief adversary. See, I thought I would sacrifice for the good of someone else. But actually, I was a pawn being sacrificed.

I look back now and see the hours put in, the love shared, the compassion extended, the kindness and confidence instilled, and see that they were all used and abused to set me up for a fall. You can see a lot of things more clearly from the bottom.

When you're at the bottom, people only see the top of your head. They don't see your heart. I heard a preacher once say that if he forgot to mention someone on the sick and shut-in list charge it to his head and not his heart. Well, I wished people could have felt and heard my heart. Instead, I had to accept the losses and find a way to get from the pit back to prominence in God's eyes and the people would see the glory of God through me again.

What they saw clearly and could measure was the fact that this devil was successful in tearing apart my family – my natural and spiritual families. Yes, my marriage was ruined. Yes, I was removed as pastor at my church. Yes, I lost my job. Yes, people I thought were friends abandoned me. Yes, I lost my varsity coaching and athletic director positions at my son's school. And the list goes on and on.

I could probably spend pages upon pages speaking about the impact on each of these areas, how many are irreconcilable, how they are damaged beyond imagination, how the ripple effect have caused much grief, heartache and headaches. But I'll briefly touch upon a couple.

My marriage wasn't in the best shape at the time my involvement with the devil was exposed. Although people on the outside looked at our marriage as a perfect, we were struggling. Despite both being ordained ministers, role models in the community and pretty good parents, she felt like I was struggling to be the husband that she dreamt of and I felt like she wasn't trying to be the wife that I knew she could be. There were times I felt like she only wanted me around because I was the father of her son. She'd say things to me that would crush me inside because what I really wanted was for her to be happy. I held a lot inside during the early years of our marriage. The pain I left at times was excruciating because I wasn't sure if she really wanted me around. But I never felt like I would be without my wife. When exposure came, we separated. Every man that I've ever counseled who was considering separating from his wife so they could work things out, I advised him not to. I felt that couples shouldn't give the devil that space to further push them apart. I knew that in separating, Tammie would find comfort in some areas being without me and I would do the same. Even after 8 years of marriage we still had differences of opinions when it came to how to keep the house, how to handle finances, whether to leave the television on or off at night, answer the phone or don't answer the phone, etc. I knew it would be much harder reconciling in separate locations. But neither of us had been this way before.

I lost my job. But that wasn't a surprise. I had lost respect for that newspaper and for many of its leaders. Some of my colleagues were great and I wish them nothing but the best. However, the way the job treated me even before my arrest was questionable at best. I knew they were setting a paper trail to dismiss me. Others felt the same way.

But the day one of my supervisors walked into the office and said he wanted to speak to me, I thought he wanted to release me from my position as a suburban reporter. But he walked me out the side door of our office into the hands of two detectives who arrested me. I wasn't surprised by the arrest because there were rumors and speculations that the police had been contacted. But I couldn't believe my job sold me out. I lost my job and the income that came along with it. But I don't miss being at the same paper that started the media frenzy because they wanted to beat the competitors with the story. I found out while I was in jail that they had suspended me.

After I was acquitted I met with them and they refused to offer me a job, saying they didn't have anything available and the information that came out at my trial makes it difficult for them to have me a part of their staff.

The first time that I saw my basketball players after my arrest was also excruciating. I saw how disappointed they were that I had let them down. They were my children. I felt like I let them down the same way I let Britt and Brad down. There wasn't much I could say or do. But I hugged them and told them that I was sorry for letting them down and that I loved them. I haven't coached since.

The impact of being removed from my pastorate wasn't immediately felt. When Bishop Carswell relieved me of my duties and responsibilities, my attention turned to dealing with my wife and my children. It was some time later that I realized I had put Bishop Carswell in a bad situation of dealing with something so weird, to say the least. I eventually thought about the members who were counting on me for spiritual guidance and leadership. I let down the members of the congregation who were assigned to me and others who also looked to me for assistance. Those I had been mentoring got hurt as well. Even months later when I returned to the church as a member only, my heart wanted to reach out to them but I couldn't because of the pending trial and because of perceptions. But many of the relationships have been lost.

Likewise, I lost relationships with many people who said they loved me and that they'd be there for me no matter what. I guess this matter was too much for them. It showed me that their words meant more than their heart. Some of these people were people I looked up to and admired. Some so-called friends turned out to be people who only benefited from what I could bring to them. And now that I was unable to bring anything to the table I no longer mattered. These people included pastors, co-workers, fellow church members, community board members, and family members. When I was bitter and angry, I wrote out each of their names and what happened. But as I grew in the process, I realized that I was only holding myself in bondage by letting them control my emotions. I read somewhere, "He who angers you, controls you." I was content to leave their names and details out because they know who they are.

## Gains

What are immeasurable are the gains that the enemy forced to come about through the process. Some can be spotted immediately such as the personal spiritual growth and maturity and the relationship with my father. But there are also gains that can't be seen such as the addition by subtraction theory. Some of the people that are no longer a part of my life, I believe God weeded out some venom that was meant to kill me. I'm better off because a lot of them are out of my life. I can speak on a number of examples, but I'll highlight a few.

## My Dad

I was 34 years old and finally heard my father say some things to me that I had been crying to hear for three decades. I'll never forget the moment that our relationship had changed forever.

I was leaving my attorney's office and I got a call from my father. He had spoken to my mother who told him that I had been arrested. He poured out how much he loved me and how he wished he could have taught me about being a man. He wished he could share with me some of his mistakes so that I wouldn't repeat them. I distinctly remember him saying he loved me four times in that one conversation. That was more than I remembered my whole life (with the exception of greeting cards).

I pulled my car to the side of the road because my crying was distracting my driving. I sat there, listening to every word that came out of his mouth. Through my sobs and whimpers, I said, "uh huh" and "yeah" like a three-year-old listening to his parent read him a bedtime story. He told me to hang in there. Keep my head up. He told me not to lie down, but stand up and fight. As if he were sitting in the passenger seat of my car, I heard his last words so vividly. "You need to be strong for your family. You need to be strong for me so that I can be strong for you."

It was a moment that defined a father-son relationship that had been dying since I convinced myself that had he been in my life as a child I would have reached my full potential. Maybe I would have been a professional baseball player. Maybe I would have pursued something else because he would have had my back and taught me what I needed to know.

He wasn't and I blamed him for everything negative in my life and that was where our relationship had been, at least to me. I called him by his first name, Tim. When I grew older and felt that it was disrespectful, I called him "Old Man," a running joke about his age and a defense mechanism that kept me from calling him dad.

But as I was faced with spending time in jail, I received something unexpected that helped me look ahead of the storm to the bright sunny day that was coming. I was finally getting a dad who loved me and was concerned for me.

From that time, we began speaking on a more regular

basis. It was what he wanted all along but I couldn't get past the wall that I built that kept him out. In talking with my father, I learned that he had loved me all along. He jogged my memory about times we spent together, places he took me and people I met while with him. He also shared with me something I didn't know… how my mother broke his heart and did some things that prevented him from being around me as much as he wanted. Now, I call him Pops.

I also gained a passion to pursue other interest. I turned my hobby of photography into a professional. I learned how to take the power out of someone else's hand for income and how to create my own. I used that same motivation to write as a way to bless others and not simply write to report the news. It was an evolution that led me to pursue all of the dreams I had to become a filmmaker and write the stories that I always said I would.

When it comes to people, I have gained a new perspective. Now, I can better discern people. I realized that everyone who says I love you, doesn't really mean it. Everyone who says they are for you, are not always for you. I can see clearly now… as the song says. It has made me sharpen my love. After I got through various stages of my process, including learning to overcome the fear of love, I utilize my gift of love with more maturity and wisdom. It has helped in my relationships with the people whom I truly love and who truly love me.

## Harvest time

While I was in jail, a friend and colleague sent Del Greco to see me and hear my case with the possibility of representing me. The friend told my family that he is willing and able to do whatever necessary to help me because I was instrumental in his renewed relationship with Jesus Christ. That was such a blessing to me because I didn't know the impact that I had on his life. But God used a tragedy to show me who my real friends are and to show me that my seeds have taken root and have created fruit.

Another friend called after I was released from jail and spoke about how I had shown such an example that the charges could not be true. They wanted to be there for me. Later, I formed a deeper relationship with someone I had ministered to. They said God told them to be there for me the same way.

## Not Guilty

God had already spoken three words to me – "not guilty" and "vindication" – long before my trial date arrived. I held onto both words during my process believing that God would remain faithful as He had throughout and that I would witness Him get the glory.

It was the day my trial began, Feb. 3, 2006. I stood in the Allegheny County Courthouse waiting for my new attorney, Art

Ettinger. There was some nervous energy but not to the magnitude of previous trips to the courthouse or across the street at family court. At the same time, there was a peace and confidence that God's stage was finally set for Him to shine.

Just before the trial was to begin, the assistant district attorney handed Ettinger a report that we had never seen before. It was a supplemental police investigation report. It generated more nerves because I knew the enemy would try to bring up something at the last minute to test my faith in God's Word. Among the items listed on the report was a new theory on how the indecent assault had occurred. It was the first we had heard anything about we had seen the report. But God turned that around quickly. The same expert that the prosecution sought for their investigation debunked the theory. The enemy had to try to come up with something else at the last minute.

What I saw was how God was turning things in His favor while extending the favor that I prayed for earlier during the 5 Requests to Be Blessed. Just before the start of the trial, the judge threw out another attempt by the prosecution, which attempted to add a second charge.

The judge saw through the prosecution's failed attempts to make something work.

He saw through all the lies and manipulation. The devil used lies and changed lies to paint a picture of me as monster. God exposed the devil for His glory.

Tammie did not have to take the stand. I did not have to take the stand. When I stood before the judge and he summarized what had taken place over the two days of the trial, my heart pounded. I was already relieved that this part of my process was coming to an end. Then I heard his words, "Not guilty. You are free to go."

More weight had lifted from my shoulders like the day I was delivered from the bondages of sin. I had gained more strength. I had gained more faith in God and His promises. I watched as He became my lawyer in that courtroom. I witnessed God turn evil into good and make a man free. I gained victory. I truly became a victor… again.

## A Warring Spirit

Finally, I learned to fight alone. You fight differently when you're on your own. You don't have someone to watch your back. You have to watch your front, back and both sides. Don't forget about watching above and below yourself. I had to find that out the hard way. At times when I felt like I had help, I was alone. When I thought someone was working for me or with me, it turned out they were really against me. Some people even thought they were helping me by doing nothing. But in actuality they left me to fend for myself. I was expecting people to be in the battle with me. Others thought they were helping by checking on me but they were planting the wrong seeds and God removed them until I was strong enough to understand what was happening. I had a trusted friend, who had been through his own challenges, call me. He said, “I know you’re feeling suicidal and you want to take your gun and shoot yourself. Or you probably just want to go to the hotel and sleep with somebody. Don’t do it!” I wasn’t suicidal. I wasn’t thinking about sleeping with anyone at that time. But those seeds could’ve have re-triggered the thinking, “Maybe things would be better off if I’m dead.” God equipped me with what I needed to persevere. He helped me become so dependent on him that no one or nothing else mattered.

# Recovering what was Lost

It would be great to get to this point and say that things turned out perfectly and we moved forward to live happily ever after. But the battle continues. There's not a day that goes by that I don't think about the things that I've been through to this point, including the process.

The "father of the modern-day men's movement" Edwin Louis Coles' quote still rings loudly, "It's easier to obtain than it is to maintain." If that's the case, it's probably harder to get back what you've lost after you've tried hard to maintain it. So you can only imagine the magnitude of commitment, strength and courage it takes to make right that which you have wronged.

With that said, I have experienced a tremendous breaking and rebuilding that forced me to look at everything that I lost. It wasn't an easy thing because forgiveness is often a hard thing to ask, as well as extend. God throws our sins into the sea of forgetfulness, but that must be where we swim. It's difficult for many people to move beyond the hurt and the pain that someone caused them because it's not fair. Sometimes people feel if they hurt, the person who hurt them should experience the same if not greater pain. A man I photographed once had a tattoo on his forehead that read: "Hurt People Hurt People." So you can basically forget about forgetting something.

But in forgiving, that's where personal restoration begins and that will open you up to wisdom on how to deal with seeking forgiveness from others. The level of sensitivity must be higher than ever expected or imagined. And, of course, when you lose something or someone dear to you, you become a little desperate. You're open to just about anything. It can be dangerous because you can set up yourself and others around you for a major explosion if it's not handled properly.

I've lost a lot. I've lost family, friends, church family, job opportunities, ministry opportunities, respect, witness, mentees, money, and the list goes on and on. So I understand how you feel if you're in a similar situation where your actions—or lack of actions—have cost you things that are dear to you. It could be your wife. Or your husband. Or your children. Or your job. You've felt hopeless and wondered why God would allow this to happen. You wonder if you will ever be able to be pleasing in God's sight. Heck, you don't even know if you will like yourself because all the things that identified you are gone and you ask yourself, "Who am I?" I've been there!

I've fought to regain some things that were lost. But in the midst of that, God showed me that He had to remove some things from me because they were hindering me from becoming the person He really wanted me to be. They were hindering me from fulfilling the purpose He set for me. At the same time, no matter how hard or long I decide to fight, restoration of some items and people are beyond my control, just like some things will be beyond your control.

That's when God wants you to buckle down and plant yourself in Him. You'll have that confidence and assurance that you've done everything in your power, in accordance with the will and word of God for good things to happen. When Tammie and I were at a distant place and I was climbing my way back into her life, I told her that no matter what, I will always love her. I wrote her a poem called, *You'll Always Be Beautiful to Me.*

## *You'll Always Be Beautiful to Me*

*You'll always be Beautiful to me.*

*No matter what, no matter where.*

*You'll always be Beautiful to me.*

*A simple message you need to hear.*

*You'll always be Beautiful to me.*

*My love will never fade.*

*You'll always be Beautiful to me.*

*That's how my heart was made.*

*You'll always be Beautiful to me.*

*Even if I can't mend your broken heart.*

*You'll always be Beautiful to me.*

*Let God, your Father, do His part.*

*You'll always be Beautiful to me.*

*No ifs, ands, or buts.*

*You'll always be Beautiful to me.*

*No matter where, no matter what.*

You'll always be Beautiful to me.

Because of where I was, I understood a lot of change needed to take place. I knew that I was in the process and I needed to change. But coming through the process, I realized that there were changes that I expected from her as well. But many things I couldn't discuss until I reached a certain plateau in my progress because I didn't want to put off my issues onto someone else or seem like I wasn't taking responsibility for my actions. Just like I made peace with God, I attempted to make peace with my wife. I had to leave the rest up to her. I just wanted to make sure that I was doing everything that I was supposed to do to be right in God's eyes and prepared to reconcile if that was going to happen. I wasn't sure that it would.

I went as far as reading books such as *His Needs, Her Needs* by Willard F. Harley Jr., *The Power of a Praying Husband* by Stormie Omartian, *Winning Your Wife Back Before It's Too*

*Late* by Gary Smalley, Greg Smalley and Deborah Smalley and *I Don't Want Delilah, I Need You!: What a Woman Needs to Know, What a Man Needs to Understand* by Bishop Eddie Long. Sometimes I would be confused in the process as one book said back off and give her time to heal and another book said go get your wife. I wanted to put my best effort forward and let my heart lead me.

There are many things that I believe will be mine again that have yet to be restored. But I believe God. I stand on His promises and the assurance that I would reap His blessings, if I just hang in there and don't faint.

I'm also reminded of Paul asking God to remove the thorn from his side. But as long as Paul was uncomfortable, he depended on God for healing of the pain. As long as the thorn was there, he was reminded of the need for a Savior. But if Paul didn't have that thorn in his flesh, maybe he wouldn't have the same need for God.

Likewise, there are many issues, situations, people, circumstances and thorns in our sides that keep us focused on God. For you, it might be struggling with cigarettes that keep you in prayer, asking God to deliver you from nicotine. But while you were thinking about kicking the nicotine habit, you remember a loved one who was diagnosed with cancer and you include him in your prayers. Maybe every business opportunity you pursue falls by the wayside and you keep praying to be a millionaire. Maybe poverty is that thorn in your side. Sure it creates some discomfort, but if it weren't there you would move to the suburbs and the people that you minister to on a daily basis on the corners, at the bars or in the barbershop might not have anyone tell them about the saving grace of Jesus Christ.

I don't know why we go through some of the things that we go through. But I believe that if we didn't, we'd miss some of the messages that God is trying to get through to us. Would I rather skip the heartache and pain, the guilt and the shame, the sorrow and blame? Absolutely! I'd love to just have the message without the costs. Technically, that's the system that God set up when he sent Jesus Christ to die for our sins. He paid the cost for everything. But because He gave us free will, we don't always heed His advice; we ignore His warnings and take the long road to get the message. Or, in some cases, we haven't learned that there is atonement from past offenses that we're responsible for.

I've learned a lot of lessons along the way, both on the short road and on the long road. I learned the principle and commandment to honor my parents right away. It didn't take switches, going without food or being outcast to realize the value in honoring them. On the flip side, how many of us were warned about touching fire before the pain of being burned taught us the lesson that we didn't hear from others?

As a result, it causes us to lose some tears, maybe some skin, hurt feelings, etc. Likewise when we fail to heed the words of the Lord, Godly advice and the examples of those before us, we tend to lose quite a bit more. I've lost quite a bit. I actually lost my life before I realized that God warned me about it 3½ years earlier.

When I turned 30 years old, God gave me the message I mentioned earlier. He asked me, "What would you do if you only had 3½ years to live and complete what I've called you to do?" The question itself was mind-boggling, let alone wondering how to respond to that. But it was a message that I began to write waiting for the opportunity to share it with someone, possibly at a men's gathering where I often encouraged men to take their rightful places in the home, in the community, and in the church.

Well, I completed the sermon but never had an opportunity to preach it. Three and a half years later, I found myself in the battle of my life and I realized that God's question to me was more than a message. It was a prophetic warning that I didn't follow through with. I also realized that I died during this battle. But just like God raised Jesus from the dead with all power in His hands, He was raising me to walk in newness of life. (Rom. 6:4-14)

The process that He was now bringing me through was about more than surviving. He was setting me up to reign with the new dimension in His power. He was giving me things that He planted 3½ years earlier, only this time they would be seasoned and matured. I was learning that there was purpose in it. There was power to gain through the process that went from death to glory.

That alone is powerful. Knowing that God raised you from the dead should be enough restoration for one to move ahead with the things of God. But God has restored much more for me and as I said, the process continues. I'm looking forward to the other miracles he's waiting to perform in my life and through my life for his glory. What hasn't been restored? I'm working on it and I'll get back to you on that.

# Giving God What's His

Fred Hammond sings a song called, "I Will Find a Way" on his project, "Somethin' 'Bout Love" that blessed me. The song begins like this:

*"I've lost some joy. I've lost some time*

*Now it feels like I will lose my mind*

*Journeyed long and lost my way*

*And now it seems 'I've lost' is all I say*

*Searching here and over there for what I've lost, where is it, I don't know*

*But I will find a way to lift up my hands*

*I will find a way to worship you, Lord*

*Though my heart is low, I'll find a way to give you praise*

*I will find a way to love you more"*

The song ends with this:

*"One thing I've not lost is the will to move ahead*

*And I kept the faith and trust in you Lord*

*And I will find a way down within myself*

*A love for you, Lord, that overflows*

*But I know that I can love you more*

*With every loss and through it all*

*But I will find a way to lift up my hands*

*And I will find a way to worship you, Lord*

*And though my life is broken I'll find a way to give you praise*

I will find a way to love you more."

I realized that my writing of praise and worship songs, poems, and just jotting down my thoughts turned out to be what God was looking for from me during various stages of my process recently.

It's hard to imagine that writing about crying all the time gives God what's His. But He said He inhabits the praises of His people. My repentance drew me closer to Him. When He delivered me, I praised and worshipped Him with songs of joy, thanksgiving and adoration. When I was in a summer season of celebration, I acknowledged Him for allowing me to experience it.

The day my trial started, I ran into a woman from Potter's House and her son. He had a court appearance before the same judge who was hearing my case. His case was postponed but as we stood in the hallway talking, God provided an opportunity for me to minister to him. He had been depressed, struggling to find a job with his case lingering over him and he felt like he was alone with no one who understood what he was going through.

I looked him in the eyes and told him that I understood exactly what he was going through. I told him that God is bringing me through this process so I could be there for people just like him. I shared with him that I have a college degree from one college, a certificate from two others and graduated from school of ministry. Yet I was bringing home less than minimum wage cleaning office buildings as I was awaiting resolution of my court case.

God has everything under control, I said. Keep your head up and keep your trust in Him and watch Him move in your favor. I told him that word was for me and yet God also gave it to me to share with others. We exchanged numbers and promised to keep in touch.

The next day, after I was acquitted, I called the teen-aged young man and shared how the favor of God was made manifest in the courtroom. God is a promise keeper, I told him.

That was almost two years after being publicly humiliated and placing so much stress on so many people. It wouldn't be the last time I asked myself this question, but I thought, "What if everything I had been through was just for this moment?"

Like I said earlier, when I got out of the Allegheny County Jail, I said I wasn't going back... not as an inmate, not to visit a family member, not to put money on anybody's books, not even to minister to members of Potter's House whom I had visited before. But it wasn't about what I had to say, it was about what God had to say.

God said that he had something for me to do at the jail. It's hard to ignore something so profound. But I admit I tried to delay a decision on it. I eventually met with the prison ministry leader and shared with him my new mandate. He arranged for me to take the training through the jail and submitted my clearances.

But what happened next was even more mind blowing. The first time I was asked to speak as a member of the prison ministry team, we were assigned to Pod 4A. Yes, the same pod that I was in wondering how I got there and vowing never to return.

I stared at Cell 214 and remembered the promises that God made to me. I watched as the door seemed to open in slow motion. As the man came through the door, for a split second I saw myself. It was a spiritual release. At that moment I was being released, set free to do what God said.

I shared my testimony with the 33 men who came down for the service. About a dozen others stood in the doorway and listened but didn't join the service. They listened as I shared how

God allowed me to be in the same situation they were in. I spoke about process and allowing God to develop and mature some things in us especially during difficult times when we feel alone, cast out and cast aside. By the time the service ended and we extended Christ to everyone gathered, we watched God move. Every one of the men gathered there stood and gave their lives to the Lord. We prayed for each of them. It was such a blessing!

On our way out of the jail, the prison ministry leader turned to me and said, "In all my years of being a part of prison ministry, I've never witnessed anything like that. I've never seen every person in the service give their lives to the Lord. God is awesome!"

I was so emotionally overwhelmed by what God had done. On the way to church after the early morning prison ministry service, I replayed everything that happened at the jail and everything that led up to that point. I remember saying again, "What if everything I had been through was just for this moment?" I watched as God got the glory from an ugly situation. There was so much more God had for me to do. He wanted to use everything that he had given me -- my gifts and talents, my experiences, and my testimonies.

I realized that God wants obedience from us now more than ever. That's why I'm going to continue to preach and teach about

His goodness and how He can make something special out of dirt. I'm going to use my filmmaking, photography and writing to be a blessing to others. I don't take that lightly. I don't minimize the fact that He gave me, of all people, a ministry of reconciliation. I owe Him. I can never fully repay Him, but I know that I owe Him.

What better way to start repaying Him than by implementing something that He revealed to me as one of my weapons. God told me that in order to combat the deeds of the flesh and sinful nature, I must operate in the fruit of the spirit and utilize the gifts of the spirit (I Cor.12). I plant this last seed with you with the prayer that it will produce... in due season.

Gal. 5:22a – *"But the fruit of the spirit is love, joy, peace, patience, kindness, goodness, faithfulness, gentleness and self-control."*

# RECOMMENDED READING


- David G. Evans, *Healed Without Scars*, (Whitaker House 2004)
- William F. Harley, Jr., *His Needs, Her Needs: Building an Affair-Proof Marriage* (Fleming H. Revell 1994)
- Stormie Omartian, *The Power of a Praying Husband* (HarvestHouse Publishers 2002)
- Gary Smalley, Dr. Greg Smalley and Deborah Smalley, *Winning Your Wife Back Before It's Too Late* (Thomas Nelson 1999)
- Frank & Ida Mae Hammond, *Pigs in the Parlor: A Practical Guide to Deliverance* (Impact Christian Books 2004)
- Doug McIntosh, *The War Within You: Overcoming the Obstacles to Godly Character* (Moody Press 2001)
- Stephen Arterburn and Fred Stoeker, *Every Man's Battle* (Waterbrook Press 2000)
- Deion Sanders, *Power, Money & Sex: How Success Almost Ruined My Life* (Word Publishing 1998)
- Floyd Flake and Donna Marie Williams, *The Way of the Bootstrapper: Nine Action Steps for Achieving Your Dreams* (HarperCollins 1999)
- T.D. Jakes, *He Motions: Even Strong Men Struggle* (G.P. Putnam's Sons 2004)

- John Paul Jackson, *Unmasking the Jezebel Spirit* (Stream Publications 2002)
- Eddie Long, *I Don't Want Delilah, I Need You* (Bethany House Publishers 2004)
- Grace Ketterman and David Hazard, *When You Can't Say "I Forgive You": Breaking the Bonds of Anger and Hurt* (NavPress 2000)
- Leanne Payne, *The Broken Image: Restoring Personal Wholeness Through Healing Prayer* (Crossway Books 1981)
- Tom Whiteman, *Victim of Love: How You Can Break the Cycle of Bad Relationships* (Pinion Press 1998)
- Rick Godwin, *Exposing Witchcraft in the Church* (Creation House 1997)

# NOTE TO THE READER

The publisher invites you to share your response to the message of this book by writing Expected End Entertainment, P.O. Box 1751, Mableton, GA 30126, or via email at expectedendentertainment@gmail.com. To order additional copies of this book or to request additional information about the author, visit us online at www.expectedendentertainment.com.